MW00640463

TAILGATE COOKBOOK

MENUS, SECRETS & STRATEGIES
TO ELEVATE YOUR PARTY GAME

By June Naylor Harris and Marshall K. Harris

GREAT TEXAS LINE PRESS

THE TEXAS TAILGATE COOKBOOK

Editor: Amy Culbertson
Cover photo: Ralph Lauer
Cover design: Kari Crane
Book design and layout: Tom Johanningmeier

ISBN 9781892588-53-1

For bulk sales and wholesale inquiries contact:
Great Texas Line Press
Post Office Box 11105, Fort Worth, TX 76110
greattexas@hotmail.com
www.greattexasline.com
817-922-8929

To see our complete list of Texas cookbooks, travel guides, sports and humor books, visit greattexasline.com.

Great Texas Line Press strives to be socially responsible, donating a portion of proceeds from several books to Texas nonprofit and cultural organizations while donating hundreds of books annually to National Public Radio stations around the state. Every effort is made to engage Texas writers, editors, illustrators, designers and photographers who have fallen victim to the newspaper industry crisis.

CONTENTS

INTRODUCTION

Texans consider it a birthright to celebrate the football season with as much merriment as possible — and what's more fun than gathering with fellow fans before the game, sharing food and drink and savoring revelry while saluting rivalries?

The beloved ritual known as the tailgate party is a time-honored tradition going back many decades, to the days when family and friends would pack a basket and a cooler with sandwiches, chips and soft drinks to enjoy from the back of the station wagon or pickup truck outside the stadium before heading in to the game. Texas didn't invent the tradition, but Texas football fans, from Longhorns to Owls, have taken to it with characteristic fervor and made it their own.

Today's tailgate parties — or, simply, tailgates, as we've come to call these pre-game festivities — can be as simple or as elaborate as you please. Here in Fort Worth at Texas Christian University, where we stage the tailgates from which this book grew, we see it all — from simple get-togethers over fast-food burgers served from the open back of an SUV to big cocktail-and-passed-appetizer affairs, complete with hired bartenders, taking place over the reach of several adjacent parking spaces. We see tailgaters hooking up big-screen TVs to watch games across the country; employing sizable sound systems to bring music to the party; and setting up huge tables, some elaborately staged and decorated, laden with food and drink. The university has even made available the option of renting large tented areas, allowing hosts who like to live large to super-size their guest lists while bringing in caterers to handle the edibles and beverages.

Our own tailgate parties are somewhere in between these two extremes: We focus on turning out great menus and bother with only a moderate amount of décor; witty conversation is all the amusement we require.

Six years ago, Marshall and I assumed the food-and-drink reins for the tailgate parties his mom and dad had been hosting for decades before each TCU home game. It was a natural progression: Marshall and I are both 1979 TCU graduates; my mother- and father-in-law are 1950s Horned Frogs alumni. Marshall and his dad are both members of the TCU Lettermen's Hall of Fame — the only father-son inductees to date — having been stars on the football teams of their respective eras. Add to that my long career as a food writer, cookbook author and recipe developer, plus Marshall's and my passion for cooking together and hosting dinner parties, and we jumped at the chance to collaborate on a weekly celebration of football and food at our alma mater.

In some ways, it's better than entertaining at home, as the party usually ends with the game's kick-off (the awkwardly lingering guest is rare) and cleanup is pretty quick, especially when a few friends stay to help out. Our guest list is a reliable combination of Mom and Dad Harris' friends and Marshall's and mine, plus a few new additions each week from the visiting team's fandom. We enjoy ourselves, no matter if rain or shine, sweltering or chilly weather, because we know that good food and drink gets every game off to a good start. So far, all our reviews have been raves.

To be fair, ample credit goes to the space itself: In front of the main entrance to the magnificent Amon G. Carter Stadium, an enormous green lawn unfolds toward Stadium Drive. A long sidewalk separates that lawn from a parallel green space adjacent to the parking lot nearest the stadium. Our parking space backs up to that green space, which is generously shaded by stately live oaks and mature crape myrtles. Even on hot days — and in Texas there are many hot Saturdays, often for half the season — we're in the shade, often in a nice breeze. Our tailgate parties are reminiscent of a lavish picnic in a lovely park.

Each season, we throw a tailgate party before every home game. That's usually six games, and at a few of our tailgates we've hosted as many as 50 to 60 guests, though 30 is more typical. The tailgate starts two hours before game time, but at least a day's worth of work goes into the preparation. We make all our dishes from scratch, and we produce a completely different menu, each with its own theme, for every tailgate. Each menu offers a main dish, two or three sides or appetizers, a dessert and a cocktail pairing. There's always water, soda, beer and wine, of course, and we make sure to take our vegetarian guests into consideration. We even have a friend who brings gluten-free treats for dessert — so there really is something for everyone.

What's most fun is coming up with the theme for each week's menu: When it's Italian, we like to feature spiedies, the grilled-meat sandwiches Marshall became fond of when living in the Northeast, along with a spread of Italian salads and our Lavender Lemon Bars. We have two different barbecue themes — Texas and Southern — and each menu reflects its heritage, right down to the desserts: Four-Berry Cobbler for Texas and Banana Pudding From Scratch for Southern. Our Chilly Saturday menu features a big pot of Texas chili, both sweet and spicy versions of our hearty Yellow Cornbread, Sunny Seven-Layer Dip with chips and Roasted-Tomato Salsa, followed by Spicy Chocolate Brownies and accompanied by Mango-Mint Margaritas. For this book, we've chosen our eight favorite menus to share with you in the coming pages.

With several seasons under our belt, we've learned a lot of strategies that spell success and a few things to steer clear of. We've gathered all those lessons into our first chapter, "Tailgate Secrets and Strategies," to spare you the trial-and-error process and to ensure that your tailgates are always in the win column.

Mostly, we serve fun at our tailgates. If our Horned Frogs are doing well, there's plenty of cheer about. But even if the team isn't bowl-bound, we're there with special food and drink for true-blue fans. And that, we think, is something to celebrate.

— June Naylor Harris with Marshall K. Harris, 2019

SECRETS AND STRATEGIES

What works, what doesn't: Troubleshooting your tailgate

Over six seasons of intensive tailgate party entertaining, we've made our share of mistakes, and every one of them has taught us lessons for future tailgates. Each season, it seems, we learn something new. Here's where we pass along our strategies for success and our hard-won tips for avoiding tailgate disasters.

PLANNING

• **Know the parameters of your tailgate area**: Your tailgate site may have restrictions about cooking equipment, whether alcohol is allowed, the number of people a space can accommodate, hours of access to the site, how trash is to be disposed of, whether electricity is available and traffic routes to and from the site.

TCU, where we tailgate, fortunately allows us a certain amount of leeway. Tabletop and portable gas grills are allowed on campus, and alcohol is OK at tailgates. Trash cans are provided. But we have to be mindful each week about traffic, as the flow of vehicles to and from the campus is strictly governed on game day, and we always plan to arrive early — at least two-and-a-half hours before kickoff. Once inside our parking lot, there is no come-and-go — so we can't forget anything. (It only happened to us once: We forgot to bring the birthday cake for an esteemed guest.)

Electricity is available near our site, but we quit using electric warming trays and slow-cookers long ago. The endless strands of extension cords were not only an eyesore but also a tripping hazard. We simply use Sterno-fueled stands with warming trays now; they are inexpensive and available in bulk at party supply stores.

• **Get your head count.** At the beginning of the season, Mom and Dad Harris send out printed invitations with the schedule of games and other info to everyone on their guest list. They touch base with everyone before each game to have a pretty good idea of who's coming; the count can vary from 30 guests up to 60.

We also maintain a Facebook page for our tailgate party, updating it weekly with our menu (including tempting photos), and we send social-media invites with RSVP options to everyone we hope will attend. Those who aren't on social media get either a text or an e-mail invitation asking for RSVPs. Yes, it takes some time, but we want a good head count before we do our grocery shopping. We don't want to overbuy or come up short.

To help those who don't know the stadium lots and locations, our invitations include a link to TCU's map page and information about which park-and-ride shuttles are available. We encourage our guests to use ride services to avoid the traffic hassles.

• **Choose a menu well in advance**. We really like being organized, so we plan our whole season of menus in August. That gives us plenty of time to tinker with recipes and shopping lists. Though we often don't know the kick-off time until a week or so before each game, we can monitor the weather forecasts and plan for warmer or cooler weather. We always stay flexible enough to sub in one of our cold-weather menus for warm-weather dishes if we hear there's a sudden cold front bearing down on us. When we get the word of an 11 a.m. kickoff, that means our tailgate starts at 9 a.m., and we substitute a brunch menu for whatever we'd originally planned.

We try to make sure each menu has a couple of easy dishes so we're not overwhelmed with prep all week long. Mindful of the lessons we've learned in practice, we avoid casseroles in general; they can dry out or even burn on the bottom if sitting over Sterno heat too long. Dishes that can keep well in big pans over heat are ideal, as are dishes for which you can set out an array of items that lets guests create their own dish. Chili, for example, fits both these requirements; it can morph into Frito pie, tacos or chili dogs, for all of which you can set out fixings and let guests build their own.

Usually we'll have a couple of side dishes to go with the main dish, as well as an appetizer to set out for guests to snack on while we're getting the rest of the goods ready to serve. We've found that arranging everything in a buffet system allows everyone to serve themselves and lets us socialize instead of filling plates for folks.

For each tailgate, we establish a theme and plan our dishes around that. To keep our menu within our chosen theme, we usually tell guests who ask "What can I contribute?" to bring whatever beer or wine they prefer to supplement the cocktail we've chosen (we always have soft drinks and water). Inevitably guests like to bring cookies or other sweets, and those are always snapped up.

PREPPING AND COOKING

• **Start a new checklist for each tailgate week**. Each game-day party is a new adventure and requires its own set of preparations. Depending on the menu, planning for the entrée typically comes first; if the main course requires marinating or advance prep, figure out if that should be done on Thursday or Friday and whether grocery shopping needs to happen Tuesday or Wednesday. Then fill in your schedule as to when you'll need to make the side dishes and appetizers; ditto for dessert and cocktail. Leave as little for game-day morning as possible.

• **Quantities:** In terms of how much to buy, it's a guessing game. Even if 40 people have replied they're coming, some will cancel last-moment, and others may show up that we hadn't expected. It happens. If we can't feed everyone, there's plenty of food at the stadium concession stands; nobody will starve! We usually average around 30 guests at our own tailgates, but we've written most of these recipes for somewhat smaller gatherings, so that they can be doubled or tripled according to your numbers.

• **Anything that can be made ahead is a plus**. Dishes that can be completely prepared ahead and brought intact in the serving dish are ideal: All we have to do at the tailgate is uncover and serve. Other dishes fare better if we prep the individual components in advance and assemble them at the party site. It's vital to know the difference. Our Three-Mustard Potato Salad on Page 29, for example, can be made at home and transported ready to serve. For salads with more acidic dressings, such as the Black-Bean Confetti Salad on Page 68 and the Grilled Sweet-Corn Salad on Page 77, you don't want to add the dressing until just before party time because the acid can break down the ingredients and make them mushy. For these, we do all the chopping and assembly of the vegetables and make the dressing at home; we keep both chilled until time to pack the truck. At the stadium, we add the dressing to the salad in a big serving bowl and let it sit for about 20 minutes while we get every-thing else ready to serve and guests sip their cocktails.

Some dishes (including most of our entrees) can be made a day or more in advance; others are better made the morning of the party. For our Smoky-Sweet Pulled Pork, on Page 36, we do the smoking a day ahead of time, shred the pork at home on the morning of the game and warm it up at the tailgate. Entrees we cook on-site include grilled specialties such as the Grilled Bratwurst and Onions With Sauerkraut on Page 84 and the Grilled Spiedies from our Festa Italiana menu on Page 92. Baked desserts that can be made the night before the game include our Spicy Chocolate Brownies (Page 109) and Lavender Lemon Bars (Page 98), but we make our Buttery Cinnamon-Pecan Monkey Bread (Page 57) and our cakes and pies on tailgate morning, when possible.

• **About grilling:** Grilling on-site is always preferable, as grilled meats simply taste their liveliest when fresh off the fire. Marshall uses a tabletop gas grill we purchased at Home Depot, as well as a gas burner for pan-sautéing veggies when needed. The tailgaters at the space right next to us bring a full-size gas grill to cook burgers each week — but not every tailgate space is structured for grilling, so be sure you know what's allowed wherever you are. Charcoal grills are the least desirable because you have burning coals to dispose of.

• **Keeping things hot:** I can't emphasize enough how useful we find the chafing pans with wire stands that hold the pans above Sterno fuel cans to keep food heated. We use the 19 1/2-by-11 1/2-by-2 1/4-inch aluminum pans and/or the half pans. For our Texas Barbecue menu, for example, we use a full pan for Marlene's Slow-Roasted Brisket, a half-pan for the Cowboy Pinto Beans and a half-pan for the Four-Berry Cobbler. For our Taco Fiesta, we use a half-pan each for the Picadillo Taco filling, the Chicken Tinga Taco filling, the tortillas and the New Mexico Green Chile con Queso.

To keep the Sterno from scorching the food and to prevent the food from drying out, here's an important trick: Place one of your long pans in the stand above the Sterno, add about an inch of water to it and then lower the pan holding the food into it for a water-insulated double pan. You can set one long pan or two half pans into it. It's imperative to keep an adequate supply of pans on hand to pack for the tailgate each week, as well as the wire stands. Don't forget to bring a couple of jugs of water to pour into those bottom pans.

• **Keeping things cold:** We buy a lot of ice each week and have quite a collection of coolers. Early on tailgate day, we head to our local Quickway and buy bags and bags of ice to chill canned soft drinks, bottled water and beer in coolers. Then we have coolers of ice for transporting the food that needs to stay chilled. If the day is a scorcher and we have something that must stay cool — such as the Herbed Sour Cream Deviled Eggs on Page 42 — we place the serving platter over a pan of ice. (We're in the shade, as I've mentioned, so I don't worry about this too much. But if the weather forecast includes 100-degree temperatures, I don't bring anything made with mayonnaise unless I know I can keep it chilled.) We also set out a small cooler of ice just for cocktails.

• **About cocktails:** I create a special cocktail each week to fit into our menu theme. For the Taco Fiesta, I make Pineapple Mojitos; for the Festa Italiana tailgate, I make a Tipsy Gypsy, similar to sangria but with rosé and a splash of Tuaca.

We found a wonderful big glass drinks dispenser for our cocktails at Bed Bath & Beyond that resembles a giant Mason jar and holds two gallons — that's about 43 (6-oz.) drinks, usually plenty for our crowd; not everyone imbibes, and some of those who do prefer a cold beer to a cocktail.

The dispenser is very heavy when full, so we usually transport the chilled-overnight cocktail ingredients in lidded plastic pitchers and mix them on site in the dispenser. I don't put ice in the dispenser because the melting ice dilutes the drinks too much. (I could probably do an ice ring in a Bundt pan at home the night before, but ... I'm already busy enough.)

For drinks that call for sparkling water, that's added to each cocktail as a splash from the bottle. I usually stick pretty close to the drinks area so I can help the guests who are serving themselves; if I have time, I'll do it for them. The little cooler with ice and an ice scoop are right there for putting ice in the glass; we use small plastic cocktail glasses that hold ice and a 6-oz. cocktail perfectly. I set garnishes (prepared ahead of time) out in bowls so everyone can add sliced lemons, limes, mint sprigs or whatever is appropriate for that week's drink.

• **Other drinks:** With the Serious Brunch menu that we serve before early kickoffs, we pack self-serve urns full of just-brewed coffee from home. We brought jugs of iced tea at first, but we realized nobody was drinking it, so we stopped. Fewer guests are drinking Cokes, so we've cut down on those a bit (or we buy the little cans) and are bringing more water these days. When we bring bottles of Topo Chico — the fabulous, super-fizzy mineral water from Mexico, always delightful when icy-cold — those are snapped up quickly.

PACKING AND TRANSPORTING

• **Start a new checklist of equipment for each tailgate**: Can you tell we love lists? Though we could probably do all of this in our sleep by now, we still keep a working checklist of every single thing we transport to the game so nothing can be forgotten. We keep large folding tables and our many folding chairs stored in the same place between games so they're easy to grab and hoist into our pickup truck bed on game-day morning. If the weather looks threatening, we have a large canopy tent we pack, as well. We're fortunate to have a tree-shaded spot, but those who don't will want a tent on hot, sunny days.

We try to pack ingredients that go together as close to each other as possible in coolers or whatever box we're using for transport. I keep a very careful checklist and cross each item off when it has actually left the house and been placed in Marshall's truck for transport to the stadium. Once we arrive, Marshall and I do all the unpacking so that we know what's been unloaded and where it is. Guests who arrive early always offer to help unpack, but we find it's easiest to steer them toward setting up the chairs and tables while we fuss with food duties.

• **Plan serving ware according to what's on the menu**. While it's easy to buy everything disposable, if you're environmentally conscious you can at least find eco-friendly disposable items, or reusable items that you can take home and wash.

We generally try to transport each dish in the vessel it'll be served in; the fewer things we have to lug, the better. If there's a way to wrap it with foil and/or plastic wrap or to use secure covers or lids, we do it. We have lots of big bowls and platters in attractive heavy-duty plastic (I love my giant purple-and-white bowls I found at Target) or ceramic (nothing that I'd be upset about breaking) that look nice at the tailgate.

We keep these and all serving utensils, such as large, heavy-duty plastic spoons and spatulas, in one storage place throughout the tailgate season. As soon as we've washed them at home after a tailgate, they go into their holding place until the next home game. Most of the durable stuff that's lasted us a few years came from Target, Marshall's or Party City.

As for forks, knives and spoons, we go with plastic — though I'd like to see us change that next year. Paper plates serve us well, as do bowls when we have chili. And, while we use only fabric napkins at home, we use paper napkins at the tailgates — I cannot imagine washing 40 or so napkins each week.

Our serving stuff doesn't vary much, and we don't spend excessive time on garnishing things, although we do like to use sprigs of herbs here and there, when it makes sense. The one thing we always do to make our table more festive: Bring along a big bunch of fresh-cut flowers in a heavy ceramic pitcher.

Here's a list to get you started:

Basics

Chairs (camp chairs are fine, but some people prefer the folding patio chair with a little table attached)

Tables (folding banquet tables — usually 6- or 8-feet-long — in heavy-duty plastic are ideal)

Tablecloths (fabric is nicer, if you don't mind doing laundry; disposable plastic is easier)

Clips or clothespins to anchor tablecloths against breezes

Metal restaurant pans and wire stands

Sterno

Electric matches

Jugs of water for warming pans

Napkins

Plates

Flatware

Drinking cups

Serving spoons and tongs

Platters and bowls

Salt and pepper shakers

Trash bags

Trash cans, if not available at your tailgate site

Self-sealing plastic bags

Wet handwipes

Foil and plastic wrap

Thermos for coffee and hot chocolate, in cold weather

Coffee creamer and sugar

Dedicated cooler or bucket for cold drinks

Ice

Ice scoop

Bottle opener for beer

Corkscrew for wine

Ice bucket for chilled wine

Special Equipment

• Cambro: At a restaurant supply store, we bought a Cambro top-loading insulated food pan carrier to keep foods hot from home to game. It's sturdy, lightweight and indispensable. At the tailgate site, we simply set up the pan stands and Sterno, then lift the pans from the Cambro onto their stands to stay warm over the Sterno.

• Portable grill: The tabletop gas grill is perfect for our purposes. It's compact, easy to pack and transport and relatively inexpensive.

• Gas burner: we sauté onions and peppers for at least a couple of our menus, and those are best served warm.

Extras

Our extras include:

A jug of freshly cut flowers for the serving table.

A two-gallon glass drink dispenser for the cocktail, plus cocktail garnishes.

A cutting board and knife for garnishes such as lemon and lime.

• **Hauling it to the tailgate site**: How anyone does this without a truck or a large SUV is a mystery to us. We have one parking space, and in-and-out access isn't allowed, so everything must be hauled in our vehicle in one trip. There's no asking friends to drive up and drop something off for us. Packing all the tables, chairs, coolers, trays of food and everything else on our checklists into the truck, along with four adults, is like working a Tetris game each week. It's taken practice, and we've learned the art of efficiency, as every square inch of space in the bed and cab is valuable. If we can pack items in other items, we do it. If the truck is too full for anyone but the driver, the rest of us must take a cab or rideshare to the game from home.

If you're new to tailgating, it wouldn't hurt to do a practice run before game day to see what you're up against and figure out where you're going to put everything. Try to keep in mind that the items you'll need to set up first should be accessible when you start to unload.

SETTING UP AND PRESENTATION

• **Assign tasks and allow at least an hour for setup**. Our tailgate parties begin two hours before kickoff. If kickoff is at 6 p.m., that means our party starts at 4 p.m., and we're on-site by 3 p.m. to begin setup. Everyone helping has a job, from setting up the folding tables and chairs, putting tablecloths on and anchoring them with clips to arranging coolers of drinks in areas that won't impede traffic flow around the food-service tables.

• **Decide where food and service items will go**. If you haphazardly place food, plates, napkins, flatware and so forth on the tailgate tables for everyone to grab, you'll surely have a chaotic party, with everyone bumping into each other. You'll need to give some thought to how best to streamline your serving flow.

We set our three folding tables up in a U shape. One side of the U holds plates, napkins and flatware, as well as the cocktail dispenser and cocktail cups. The entrée goes at the short middle table of the U. If we're grilling, guests are given the brats or other grilled item there; otherwise, guests serve themselves from warming trays. Guests continue to the other leg of the U for all the side dishes, condiments and desserts.

BREAKING DOWN

• **When the party's over**: Most guests head into the stadium before kick-off, and we begin cleanup then. Now and then we have friends who came for the fellowship but don't have tickets for the game, and they'll help us clean up. On especially nice evenings, we've sat outside the stadium during the game and watched it on our neighbor's large TV setup. In fact, lots of our tailgate neighbors stay outside during the game; we have a beautiful setting, and the neighbors next to us have strung up white lights in the live-oak tree, so it's a lovely way to spend an evening outdoors. In these situations, lots of grazing goes on during the game.

If there are leftovers that will make for good eating the next day, we stash those in plastic bags and in coolers, but our goal is to plan so well we don't waste anything. To repack the truck, we simply do it the way we did that morning. If you're new at this, take photos of how you got everything packed before you leave home for the stadium, so you can do the same thing post-tailgate.

AND FINALLY

If you're just getting started at this tailgate thing, go easy on yourself. Start small. Get lots of people to pitch in. You'll have fun, no matter what — and that's the point. As with anything else, you get a lot better with practice.

EIGHT TAILGATES: MENUS AND RECIPES

TEXAS BARBECUE

Texas Barbecue Sauce
Marlene's Slow-Roasted Brisket
Slow-Cooker Cowboy Pinto Beans
Three-Mustard Potato Salad
Refrigerator Pickles With a Kick
Four-Berry Cobbler With Sugared Biscuit Crust
Cocktail: The Back Nine

There's probably a written rule somewhere dictating that barbecue must be served at a tailgate at least once per season. In Texas, few people can get enough barbecue, so we feature it at our tailgates twice each season, starting with traditional Texas flavors and continuing with the Southern-style menu in the following chapter.

The menu on the next few pages includes a brisket that's a little less sweet in the sauce than its Southern counterpart, along with other complementary components. While this brisket isn't smoked over a wood fire, we promise you'll get rave reviews. It's easily the most-requested meat among our tailgate guests.

TEXAS BARBECUE SAUCE

I've tweaked my own mom's recipe over the years to come up with a barbecue sauce that strikes the perfect balance between sweet and spicy. If you like a little extra fire but your guests aren't as brave, just add some Crystal (or another good Louisiana hot sauce) to the portion on your plate.

Yield: 1 pint

14-oz. bottle ketchup
1/2 cup apple-cider vinegar
1/4 cup spicy brown mustard
1/4 cup Worcestershire sauce
1 1/2 tablespoons molasses
3 teaspoons granulated garlic
1 to 2 teaspoons chili powder, as desired
Sea salt, to taste

In a medium saucepan, combine ketchup, vinegar, mustard, Worcestershire sauce, molasses, garlic granules and chili powder; bring to a gentle boil, then reduce to a simmer. Simmer mixture, uncovered, for 10 to 15 minutes. Remove from heat and allow to cool. Stir, taste and add salt as needed. Store chilled; for serving, bring to room temperature or reheat gently.

MARLENE'S SLOW-ROASTED BRISKET

Marshall's mom, Marlene Harris, began making this slow-roasted brisket decades ago, and it's a signature dish for which family members would walk over burning coals to get just one bite. This foolproof staple comes together easily, but you'll need to plan ahead — it cooks low and slow in the oven. Seasonings and sauce are key touches for this falling-apart-tender beef. Serve with hamburger buns or tortillas. If you have leftovers, take 'em home and stuff 'em into a baked potato for another meal.

Yield: 10 to 12 servings

1 tablespoon sea salt
1 tablespoon granulated onion powder
1 tablespoon granulated garlic
1 tablespoon celery salt
1 tablespoon black pepper
2 teaspoons sugar
1 (5- to 6-pound) beef brisket, trimmed
3 tablespoons Worcestershire sauce
3 tablespoons Liquid Smoke
1 cup Texas Barbecue Sauce (see previous recipe)

Make rub by combining all seasonings with sugar, mixing well. Rub evenly over surface of brisket. Place brisket on a sheet of heavy foil big enough to completely enclose it and brush all over with Worcestershire sauce and Liquid Smoke. Wrap tight in foil and refrigerate overnight.

In the morning, place wrapped brisket in a large, heavy pan and bake at 250° for 5 hours.

Remove pan from oven, leaving the oven on. Unwrap brisket and use a ladle to transfer as much of the drippings as you can into a bowl. Stir the cup of Texas Barbecue Sauce into the drippings. Mix well and pour over the brisket. Loosely rewrap brisket with foil and return to oven for 30 minutes.

Remove from oven, discard excess liquid and allow brisket to rest at room temperature for at least 15 minutes before shredding. For serving, offer hamburger buns so that guests can make sandwiches, with a container of Texas Barbecue Sauce alongside for ladling over the shredded brisket.

SLOW-COOKER COWBOY PINTO BEANS

My family has loved a good pot of pintos, with cornbread on the side, since I can remember. This recipe geared to a slow cooker or Instant Pot makes the work easy. Smoked pork is a traditional seasoning for beans, but if you have vegetarians among your guests, the beans will be tasty enough without it.

Yield: 12 to 14 servings

1 1/2 pounds dried pinto beans
4 cloves garlic, roughly chopped
1 medium yellow onion, diced
4 thick slices smoked bacon, diced, optional
Sea salt and black pepper, to taste
2 tablespoons freshly ground chile powder, or to taste, optional
  (see note)

Soak beans in cold water overnight; in the morning, drain, rinse and transfer to a slow cooker. Add just enough water to cover; stir in garlic, onion, bacon (if using), salt and pepper. Cook on low for 4 to 5 hours, just until beans are tender.

You can also use the quick-soak method: Bring beans to a boil in salted water and boil for 10 minutes. Drain and let cool slightly; transfer to a slow cooker and proceed with recipe.

NOTE: If you don't have a good source for freshly ground chile powder near you, check out the online offerings at Pendery's, open in Fort Worth since 1870: penderys.com.

THREE-MUSTARD POTATO SALAD

Some folks prefer a mustard-based potato salad, and we are among them. This one is loaded with flavor, thanks to Marshall's homemade bread-and-butter pickles — but the pickles you get at the grocery store will work fine, too. We're big fans of those from Best Maid, based in Fort Worth but sold widely in stores and online, bestmaid-products.com.

Yield: 12 servings

6 to 8 medium russet potatoes, peeled and chopped into 1-inch pieces
3 large celery stalks, tops removed, diced
3/4 cup chopped green onion, white and green parts
3/4 cup finely diced bread-and-butter pickles
1 cup sour cream
2 tablespoons yellow mustard
1 tablespoon brown mustard (either spicy or mild)
1 tablespoon Dijon mustard
Sea salt and black pepper, to taste

Cover potatoes with cold water in a large pot; bring to a boil, then reduce to a simmer. Simmer, covered, 10 minutes or just until potatoes are tender. Don't let the potatoes get mushy!

Drain potatoes and allow to cool. Combine potatoes and all remaining ingredients in a large bowl and mash with a potato masher or large fork until almost smooth, allowing some smaller chunks to remain for texture. Chill until serving time.

REFRIGERATOR PICKLES WITH A KICK

The beautiful garden Marshall has created in our backyard goes crazy each summer with cucumbers and jalapeños. There've been weeks when I've seen him put on his canning apron and pickle cucumbers by the bushel and still not be able to keep up with the garden's pace. We stumbled on a great quick-pickling recipe that gives you overnight pickles, so we can enjoy the fruits of his labor while the canned versions are undergoing their slower transformation. It utilizes both vinegar and canning-and-pickling salt, available in most grocery stores, in the curing process. Fortunately, I crave pickles like mad and consume them with every kind of sandwich, smoked meat and pot of beans I can think of. These are great with any kind of barbecue, I promise. Just remember to allow 24 hours for them to be ready to eat. If some in your crowd don't like heat, you can make half the batch without the jalapeños, or leave them out entirely (the jalapeños, not your timid friends).

Yield: 4 (1-pint) jars

4 large cucumbers
3 tablespoons canning-and-pickling salt, divided

2 large red onions, peeled and trimmed
4 large carrots, peeled and trimmed
2 to 3 jalapeño peppers, optional
8 fresh dill sprigs
2 cups apple-cider vinegar (5% acidity)
1/2 cup sugar
1/4 cup fresh lemon juice
2 teaspoons dill seeds

Score each cucumber lengthwise all over with fork tines (this is optional, but it takes only a couple of minutes and makes the pickles look prettier). Trim ends and slice cucumbers into 1/4-inch-thick slices. Spread out slices in a large colander in the sink and sprinkle with 1 1/2 tablespoons of the pickling salt. Allow excess liquid to drain for 30 minutes; then rinse slices and pat them dry.

Meanwhile, slice onion and carrots 1/4-inch-thick into a large bowl. Make a lengthwise slit in each jalapeño and scrape out as many of the seeds as you can with the point of your knife. Slice jalapeños very thinly into the bowl. Add cucumber slices and toss all together to mix well.

Place 2 dill sprigs in each of 4 (1-pint) canning jars. Pack vegetable mix into jars, leaving a 1/2-inch headspace. In a saucepan, bring vinegar, sugar, lemon juice, dill seeds and remaining 1 1/2 tablespoons of pickling salt to a boil over medium-high heat, stirring until sugar and salt dissolve. Turn off heat.

Extreme temperature changes can cause glass to break, so you want to raise the temperature of your jars before pouring in the hot vinegar mixture. You can do this by capping the jars and running very hot water over them or sitting the capped jars in a sinkful of very hot water (don't let any water get into the jars).

Once jars are warmed up, remove lids and pour hot vinegar mixture over vegetables; then replace lids. Chill for 24 hours before serving. These keep well in the fridge for up to 3 weeks.

FOUR-BERRY COBBLER WITH SUGARED BISCUIT CRUST

You can whip up a drop or rolled biscuit dough and use a mini biscuit cutter to make small rounds, if that's your preference. But the canned variety works just fine; if you're pressed for time, this is the way to go. When those berry juices bubble up and mingle with the sparkling sugar crystals atop the browned crust, I'll guarantee that no one will care whether a can was involved.

Yield: 12 to 14 servings

4 tablespoons butter, melted, divided
2 cups fresh blueberries
2 cups fresh strawberries, hulled and cut into quarters
1 cup fresh blackberries
1 cup fresh raspberries
1 tablespoon fresh lemon juice
1/2 cup sugar
3 tablespoons cornstarch
8 canned buttermilk biscuits, each cut into quarters
2 tablespoons coarse sugar (see note)

Preheat oven to 350° and use 1 tablespoon of the butter to grease a 9-by-12-inch casserole dish.

Toss berries with lemon juice in a large bowl.

Whisk together sugar and cornstarch in a small bowl, then sprinkle the sugar mixture over the berries and toss to combine well. Turn berries into the buttered casserole dish.

Arrange biscuit dough quarters evenly on top of berries. Brush biscuits with remaining 3 tablespoons melted butter and sprinkle with coarse sugar. Bake about 45 minutes, or until biscuit crust is nicely browned and berries are bubbling.

NOTE: Any coarse sugar will do; options include decorating sugar, sanding sugar, icing sugar and turbinado sugar, all available in most baking aisles.

THE BACK NINE

Everyone loves an Arnold Palmer, that easy mix of freshly brewed iced tea and handmade lemonade. When you want to give it some oomph, add some hooch. This is the favorite among almost all the cocktails we've served at the tailgate; we like bourbon in it but guests seem to prefer vodka. Either way, you'll have happy guests.

Yield: 1 gallon, or about 21 (6-oz.) cocktails

5 cups vodka
5 cups freshly brewed iced tea, cooled
3 cups water
2 cups fresh lemon juice
1 cup mint simple syrup (recipe below)
2 thinly sliced lemons
10 mint sprigs, plus more for garnish

Mint simple syrup: In a saucepan, combine 1 1/4 cups water, 1 cup sugar and several fresh mint sprigs. Bring to a gentle boil and reduce to a simmer, stirring until sugar dissolves. Remove from heat and cool completely. Discard mint sprigs. Store, covered, in refrigerator until ready to use.

To make the cocktails, combine all ingredients and chill. Serve in glasses filled with ice, garnished with more fresh mint, if you like.

●●●

Logistics: Shred the brisket before leaving home, wrapping it securely for transport to keep it from drying out. If your tailgate site has convenient electrical outlets, you can transport and serve the beans in the slow cooker, but our on-site tailgate scenario doesn't include electrical components, so we transfer the beans to one of our foil pans that can be kept hot over Sterno for transporting and serving.

Don't forget: Buns and hot sauce for the brisket — we offer both hamburger and slider buns, as some people, both young and old, prefer small sandwiches — and fresh mint sprigs for the cocktail garnish, if you're using them. We keep our fresh herbs perky by wrapping them in a damp paper towel and tucking the bundle into a plastic bag.

SOUTHERN BARBECUE

Smoky-Sweet Pulled Pork
Duo of Barbecue Sauces
  Memphis-Style Barbecue Sauce
  Carolina-Style Mustard Sauce
Tart and Tangy Slaw
Marlene's Garden Potato Salad
Herbed Sour-Cream Deviled Eggs
Banana Pudding From Scratch
Cocktail: Moscow Frog

The kind of barbecue you like says a lot about where your people call home. Barbecue styles vary radically from the Carolinas and Georgia to Alabama and Mississippi, Tennessee and Kansas City — and, finally, to Texas. While we love our beef brisket in Texas, you won't find much brisket in 'Q joints east of here. Pork is king in the South, whether you're talking about a rack of ribs or pulled pork. The latter has become one of the happiest middle grounds these days: Though you wouldn't have found pulled pork on a Texas smokehouse menu 20 years ago, it's readily available at most barbecue joints in the Lone Star State now. We built this tailgate around pulled pork as the centerpiece, as it's such a crowd-pleaser — Marshall doubles down on the flavor with both a marinade *and* a rub — and so easy to make for a big gathering. The rest of the menu consists of items with distinctive Southern charm.

SMOKY-SWEET PULLED PORK

Boston butt is a common name for pork butt, which is actually pork shoulder. It's the most popular cut for pulled pork, having become a Texas barbecue mainstay over the last decade or so. Marshall makes a wonderfully tender version in our Big Fake Egg (the Big Green Egg knockoff we found at Sam's Club for half the price of the famous brand). It's a dependably easy recipe, too. Plan to devote time to an overnight marinating process and a low, slow smoking period. Just watch your temperature and you'll do fine. The rule of thumb is roughly an hour per pound in the smoker at about 225°, until the meat's internal temperature is 200° degrees. Always allow the meat to rest, wrapped in foil, for about an hour after you've pulled it from the smoker. Make sure to check the directions that came with your smoker before proceeding. You'll need a good supply of hardwood charcoal briquettes — hickory, mesquite, pecan or oak. You can serve pulled pork on buns, as is customary, or in tortillas (some folks like corn tortillas, some like flour, so we provide both).

Yield: 14 to 16 servings

Seasoning rub:
2 cups firmly packed dark-brown sugar
1/2 cup coarse sea salt
2 tablespoons smoked paprika
2 tablespoons ground mustard
2 tablespoons garlic granules
1 tablespoon coarsely ground black pepper

Marinade:
2 cups apple juice
2 cups Dr Pepper

2 cups apple-cider vinegar
1 cup seasoning rub (see above)

Pork:
10-pound bone-in Boston butt

Seasoning rub: Stir all ingredients together until mixed thoroughly. Store in airtight container.

Marinade: Mix all ingredients together in an oversized self-sealing plastic bag large enough to hold the liquid and the pork.

Pork: Add pork butt to bag with marinade. Seal well and allow to marinate overnight in the refrigerator, turning every few hours. (Marshall likes to ramp up his production, injecting the pork butt with the marinade before sealing it into the bag. If you'd like to try this, meat injectors are widely available for as little as $5 at Walmart, or an average of $10 to $20 on Amazon and about $20 at Home Depot.)

When ready to cook, prepare smoker according to your equipment's instructions. Discard marinade and pat pork dry with tea towels. Coat the entire surface of the pork with the seasoning rub and allow the pork to sit at room temperature while the smoker comes to proper heat. Smoke as per instructions, typically an hour per pound. Remember to allow pork to rest at room temperature, covered in foil, before shredding, using two forks.

Serve with sandwich buns or warm tortillas.

A DUO OF BARBECUE SAUCES

Why two? Because it's too hard to decide which is better. One is a little sweeter, made with a tomato base, like you might find in Memphis. The other is mustard-based, a popular choice in the Carolinas. To be honest, I like to put a little of both together. And if it's handy, I'll add a shot of hot sauce, too — a little heat with tangy and sweet never hurts. I like to decant the sauce into glass swing-top bottles for serving; plastic squeeze bottles don't look as cool but work really well too.

MEMPHIS-STYLE BARBECUE SAUCE

The combination of cider and white balsamic vinegar with Coca-Cola and molasses (we like the Steen's brand from Louisiana) produces a tart sauce tempered with a hint of sweetness. Adjust the cayenne pepper as desired.

Yield: 3 cups

2 tablespoons vegetable oil
1 yellow onion, chopped
3 cloves garlic, minced
10.75-oz. can tomato puree
1 tablespoon tomato paste
3/4 cup apple-cider vinegar
3/4 cup white balsamic vinegar
1/2 cup dark molasses
1/4 cup Worcestershire sauce
1/4 cup Coca-Cola

1 tablespoon yellow mustard
1 teaspoon sweet paprika
1/2 to 1 teaspoon cayenne pepper, as desired
Sea salt to taste

Heat oil in a medium skillet over medium-high heat; add onion and sauté until translucent, about 4 to 5 minutes. Add garlic and stir another minute or so. Stir in all remaining ingredients and bring to a gentle boil; reduce heat and simmer, uncovered, about 15 minutes, stirring occasionally. Cool slightly.

Using an immersion or traditional blender, puree sauce until smooth. To store, refrigerate in a covered container; serve warm or at room temperature.

CAROLINA-STYLE MUSTARD SAUCE

My secret to making this sauce sing is Pickapeppa Sauce, that fabulous and timeless condiment from Jamaica found in just about any grocery store. Its blend of tomato, sugar, vinegar and mango gives great punch to this sauce.

Yield: 3 cups

1 1/2 cups yellow mustard
1 cup apple-cider vinegar
3/4 cup dark-brown sugar
1/4 cup honey
2 tablespoons Pickapeppa Sauce
Sea salt and black pepper to taste

Combine all ingredients in a medium saucepan over medium-high heat. Bring to a low boil, then reduce heat to low and allow to simmer, uncovered, with an occasional stir, for 20 minutes. Cool and chill overnight in a covered container. Serve at room temperature.

TART AND TANGY SLAW

The best foil to that smoky pulled pork is a vinegar-based slaw. Whether you pile the slaw atop your sandwich or just eat it alongside, the flavor complement is hard to beat. If you're pressed for time, you can buy already-chopped cabbage and shredded carrots.

Yield: 12 to 14 servings

1 head green cabbage, cored and thinly sliced
1/2 head purple cabbage, cored and thinly sliced
8 carrots, peeled and chopped in food processor
8 green onions, trimmed and thinly sliced (green and white parts)
1 cup apple-cider vinegar
1/4 cup honey
1/2 cup extra-virgin olive oil
3 teaspoons garlic granules
2 teaspoons celery seeds
Sea salt and coarsely ground black pepper, to taste

Toss the sliced cabbages, carrots and onions together in a large bowl. To make the dressing, in a separate bowl, whisk the remaining ingredients together for 2 minutes, until the mixture emulsifies a bit. Drizzle the dressing over the veggies and toss well to combine. Serve chilled or at room temperature.

MARLENE'S GARDEN POTATO SALAD

For those loving a mayonnaise base and lots of veggie crunch, this is the perfect potato salad — another specialty from Marshall's mom, Marlene Harris. Keys to this one are patience (there's a lot of chopping and slicing) and a gentle turn of the ingredients with the mayo; you want the consistency as chunky as possible. "Do not mash the potatoes," advises Marlene, "that's for mustard-onion Texas potato salad." (That would be my Three-Mustard Potato Salad on Page 29.) Marlene also says to adjust the amount of mayonnaise, veggies, salt and pepper to your preference and to be sure it sits overnight in the fridge to let flavors develop.

Yield: 12 to 14 servings

3 pounds potatoes, scrubbed (about 8 medium)
2 large cucumbers, peeled, seeded and cut into very small cubes
3 teaspoons salt
1 1/2 bunches radishes, trimmed and thinly sliced
1 1/2 bunches green onions, trimmed and thinly sliced (green and
   white parts)
5 to 6 stalks celery, trimmed and thinly sliced
10 hard-boiled eggs, peeled and sliced, divided
1 cup mayonnaise, or as much as desired
Salt and pepper to taste
A few dashes paprika

Cover potatoes in a large pot with cold water. Bring to boil over medium-high heat, then reduce heat to low; cover and simmer till tender, about 15 minutes. Drain and cool to room temperature.

Meanwhile, spread cucumber cubes on a tea towel and sprinkle with 3 teaspoons salt; allow to sit for about 10 minutes. Now cover them with another tea towel, place a cookie sheet over the towel and press down firmly to expel as much excess liquid from the cucumbers as possible; you don't want a watery potato salad. Transfer cucumber cubes to a colander or strainer and rinse with running water to remove salt. Pat dry thoroughly and transfer to large bowl.

When potatoes are cool enough to handle, peel and cut into 3/4-inch cubes; add to cucumbers in bowl, along with radish slices, green onion, celery slices and 8 of the sliced eggs. Toss very gently with mayonnaise and salt and pepper to taste.

Arrange remaining sliced eggs on top of salad and sprinkle with paprika. Cover and chill overnight. Serve cool.

HERBED SOUR-CREAM DEVILED EGGS

A favorite recipe from Martha Stewart inspired these eggs. Using sour cream instead of mayonnaise results in a tart filling that has a little more body. Vary the herbs, if you like, switching out cilantro for parsley or basil for dill.

Yield: 16 servings

8 large eggs
1/2 cup sour cream
1 teaspoon grainy Dijon mustard
1 1/2 teaspoons white balsamic vinegar
Coarse salt and freshly ground pepper to taste
1 teaspoon chopped fresh flat-leaf parsley

1 teaspoon chopped fresh dill, plus fronds for garnish
1 teaspoon finely chopped fresh chives, plus snipped chives for
   garnish

In a large saucepan, cover eggs with water by an inch or two. Bring to a boil over medium-high heat. Cook, gently stirring as water begins to boil, 2 minutes, counting from the time the water begins to boil gently (stirring helps keep yolks centered). Cover pan, remove from heat and let stand 10 minutes; then transfer eggs to an ice-water bath and let cool for 5 minutes.

Peel eggs and halve lengthwise. Remove yolks carefully to a bowl with a small spoon and set white halves aside. Mash yolks with sour cream, mustard and vinegar; season to taste with salt and pepper and gently stir in herbs.

If you want to pipe the filling into the egg whites, transfer yolk mixture to a pastry bag fitted with an open-star tip and pipe mixture into whites, filling to 1/2 inch over surface. Or just use a small spoon to fill the egg-white cavities. Garnish with extra herbs. Eggs can be refrigerated in an airtight container.

BANANA PUDDING FROM SCRATCH

Anyone can make banana pudding from a box mix, but the artificial flavors don't suit my taste — even when you try to mask them with a lot of banana slices. Why not take a little extra time and make the real thing? Your guests will taste the difference and lavish you with praise. Be sure to use pure vanilla extract (not vanilla flavoring!), such as the Watkins or Nielsen-Massey brand Madagascar vanilla.

Serve in mini Mason jars (the 4-oz. size), topped with whipped cream and extra cookies. And about those cookies: Shortbread are the best bet; they hold up well when covered by bananas, pudding and whipped cream, but some folks can accept only vanilla wafers in their 'nana pudding.

Yield: 16 mini-servings (4 oz.)

3/4 cup sugar
1/4 cup all-purpose flour
Pinch sea salt
3 large egg yolks
2 3/4 cups whole milk
1 1/2 teaspoons pure vanilla extract
30 shortbread cookies or 45 vanilla wafers, divided
8 bananas, divided
3/4 cup whipping cream
1 tablespoon sugar

Make custard: Combine sugar, flour and salt in a large, heavy saucepan. In a large bowl, lightly beat egg yolks and then whisk in milk. Pour the egg-milk mixture into the saucepan and cook over medium-low heat, stirring constantly, until smooth and thick. Remove from heat and stir in vanilla.

Set aside 16 of the cookies to use for garnish at serving time. Coarsely crumble the rest.

Peel and slice 6 of the bananas. Cover bottoms of 16 mini Mason jars (the wide-mouth 4-oz. size) with a layer of crumbled cookies and add a layer of banana slices. Pour custard over that layer and repeat process with more crumbled cookies, banana slices and custard, finishing with a layer of crumbled cookies. Cover jars with lids and chill thoroughly.

Just before it's time to leave for the tailgate, whip cream with sugar, using an electric mixer. Transport whipped cream in a tightly covered plastic container in your cooler. Take along the 2 reserved bananas and the 16 whole cookies as well.

At the tailgate site, peel and slice bananas (you'll need 16 slices). Whip the cream once more with a whisk to re-incorporate if separated. Uncover jars, top each with a big dollop of whipping cream, a slice of banana and a cookie.

MOSCOW FROG

What adult beverage has seen a greater rise in popularity these past few years than the Moscow Mule? The combination of ginger, mint and lime is really refreshing, and the variations thereof — usually a switching-out of citrus flavors — are easy to produce. Our favorite ginger beer brands are Fever Tree and Q Drinks; both have sparkling, crisp flavor, aren't overly sweet and are designed for mixing. For this tailgate specialty, we just add a hint of blueberry-pomegranate juice to create a purple-hued libation. It's perfect for our TCU celebrations and looks beautiful in our big glass drink dispenser. Be sure to have plenty of lime wheels and fresh mint sprigs for garnish on hand.

Yield: About 20 (6.5-oz.) cocktails

3 3/4 cups vodka
1 1/4 cups freshly squeezed lime juice
1 1/4 cups bottled blueberry-pomegranate juice

10 to 12 (6.8-oz) bottles or (7.5-oz) cans ginger beer
Ice
Lime wheels for garnish
Mint sprigs for garnish

Combine vodka, lime juice and blueberry-pomegranate juice. Refrigerate overnight to chill well.

At serving time, transfer the mixture into drinks dispenser. Pour short glasses about halfway full, add ice, top with ginger beer, stir and garnish with lime and mint.

•••

Logistics: To transport and serve the deviled eggs, you can find heavy plastic covered containers made specifically for deviled eggs at purveyors like Bed, Bath & Beyond, Wal-Mart and Amazon.

You'll want to pack the egg, slaw and potato salad containers in a large cooler with ice and leave them in the cooler until serving time.

Shred the pork at home (ideally the morning of the tailgate), wrapping it securely in heavy foil to preserve moisture, and transport in a Cambro to keep warm.

Set up your serving station with thought: The order we find most effective is buns/tortillas, followed by pulled pork, sauces, slaw and then the other sides, followed by dessert.

When you uncover the pudding jars at the tailgate to add the whipped cream and garnishes, be sure to tuck the lids away somewhere secure so you can take them home along with the empty jars to be washed and reused. It wouldn't hurt to designate a spot for folks to return their empty jars.

Don't forget: Sandwich buns (we offer both burger and slider mini-buns) or tortillas for the pulled pork; a bottle of your favorite hot sauce for fire-lovers; a whisk for the whipped cream, the whole bananas (and a knife to slice them) and cookies for the pudding garnish; lime and mint for cocktail garnishes.

SERIOUS BRUNCH

Tater Tot Breakfast Bake
Pear-Cherry Compote With Yogurt and Homemade
  Nutty Granola
Marshall's Buttermilk Biscuits
Southern Sausage Gravy
Fruit Salad With Lemon-Lavender Simple Syrup
Buttery Cinnamon-Pecan Monkey Bread
Cocktails:
  Janie's Perfect Bloody Marys
  A Mimosa Bar

Each season, we greet news of an 11 a.m. kickoff with a combination of glee (we love a great brunch) and a smidge of grumpiness (it makes for a very early Saturday). So I like to subtitle this tailgate "Good Morning, Sunshine!," trying not to layer on the sarcasm, and hope it's a pretty day.

When the game starts at 11, that means our tailgate start time is no later than 9 a.m., which means we're baking biscuits and monkey bread and making sausage gravy by 6:30 a.m., packing the truck and checking all the to-do items off the list by 7:30. On a Saturday.

We pick up Marshall's parents en route to the stadium and hope to be setting up by 8:30 a.m., providing early arrivals with a cup of coffee or a Bloody Mary as soon as possible. We unload our hot food, set up the chafing dishes and light Sternos as soon as we can.

If we've made time to do so, we stop at Dale's Donuts No. 9, one of Fort Worth's favorite little bake shops, to buy a dozen doughnuts and sausage rolls for folks to snack on while we're getting the tailgate operation ready. Once everything is set up, we relax, sip an eye-opener of our own and heave a sigh of relief.

TATER TOT BREAKFAST BAKE

Yes, this could be considered a casserole. Yes, we advised against casseroles earlier in the book. For the purposes of the brunch tailgate, however, you're not likely to have the pan warming over the heating element for hours on end. The food will be gone in less than 2 hours, so there's less worry about it drying out too quickly. Setting the warming pan inside a pan of water also guards against scorching. And, honestly, who can resist tots? If you have vegetarians, make a half-pan with bacon and another without. Best of all: Make this the night before and bake early in the morning, while you are pulling together the rest of the menu.

Yield: 16 servings

1 pound bacon slices
2 (16-oz.) bags frozen tater tots, unthawed
2 pounds mushrooms, cleaned and sliced 1/4-inch thick
2 bunches green onions (both green and white parts), trimmed and chopped
1 3/4 cups half-and-half
2 teaspoons granulated garlic

2 teaspoons dried Italian seasoning
Salt and pepper to taste
8 large eggs, beaten well
2 cups grated pepper jack cheese, divided
1 cup grated sharp white cheddar cheese, divided

Cook the bacon in a skillet over medium heat until crisp; drain bacon on paper towels and reserve about 1 tablespoon of drippings in skillet.

Meanwhile, spray the interiors of 2 (11 3/4-by-9 1/4-inch) baking pans with nonstick cooking spray. Line the bottoms of the pans with the frozen tater tots, breaking up any clumps of tots that have frozen together.

Reheat the 1 tablespoon reserved bacon drippings in the skillet over medium-high and sauté the mushrooms until tender, stirring frequently, about 5 minutes. With a slotted spoon, transfer mushrooms to the pans, dividing them equally. Crumble bacon and scatter chopped green onions on top.

In a large bowl, whisk together half-and-half, garlic, seasonings, eggs and half the cheeses. Pour mixture over the tots in the pans and scatter remaining cheese on top. Cover with foil and refrigerate overnight.

In the morning, let pans come to room temperature while oven heats to 350°. Bake, covered with foil, for 30 minutes, then uncover and bake another 20 to 25 minutes. Cut into squares to serve.

PEAR-CHERRY COMPOTE WITH YOGURT AND HOMEMADE NUTTY GRANOLA

Each year, we find that more guests are eager for something a tad lighter to eat — particularly in the morning. We're seeing more vegetarians among our guests, too, as time goes on. Our response: offering a favorite vanilla yogurt in individual serving packages (I'm fond of the Noosa brand, but I'm also a big fan of the thick Icelandic yogurt-like skyr), to be combined with our Pear-Cherry Compote and Homemade Granola as each guest sees fit. The fruit compote is also delicious on Marshall's Buttermilk Biscuits, below — as well as on pancakes, waffles, pound cake and ice cream anytime, so go ahead and make an extra batch. The granola is a great snack for kids at the tailgate, too.

PEAR-CHERRY COMPOTE

Yield: 4 cups

4 Bosc or Red Anjou pears, peeled, cored and chopped
3/4 cup dried cherries
1/2 cup plus 2 tablespoons cranapple juice
2 tablespoons light-brown sugar
1 1/2 tablespoons apple-cider vinegar
1 teaspoon ground cinnamon
1/2 teaspoon sea salt

In a medium saucepan over medium heat, combine chopped pears, dried cherries, cranapple juice, brown sugar and vinegar. Stir occasionally, allowing mixture to come to a gentle boil. Reduce heat to simmer and cook about 5 to 10 minutes, uncovered, allowing mixture to reduce by half. Season with cinnamon and salt, stirring well. Remove from heat and cool to room temperature. Chill until serving time.

HOMEMADE NUTTY GRANOLA

You can use any type of dried fruit, or a mix, or none at all, since the compote above provides a fruit component.

Yield: 5 cups

3 cups old-fashioned rolled oats (not instant!)
1/2 cup chopped pecans
1/2 cup chopped walnuts
1/2 cup sliced almonds
1/2 cup raw pepitas (pumpkin seeds) or sunflower seeds
2 teaspoons ground cinnamon
1 teaspoon sea salt
Pinch ground nutmeg
3 tablespoons raw honey
2 tablespoons coconut oil or avocado oil
1 cup chopped dried fruit, preferably unsweetened, optional

Heat oven to 300° and line a large rimmed cookie sheet with parchment paper.

In a large bowl, combine oats, nuts and seeds, cinnamon, salt and nutmeg. Mix well. Drizzle honey and oil over the mixture and toss well.

Turn mixture onto the lined cookie sheet and spread evenly. Bake for 15 minutes, then mix all ingredients well with a wooden spoon and return to oven for another 15 minutes, or just until the mixture is browning evenly. (Keep an eye on it; you may need to rotate the pan if it's browning unevenly.) Allow granola to cool and mix in dried fruit, if desired. Store in an airtight container at room temperature for up to 1 week.

MARSHALL'S BUTTERMILK BISCUITS

Marshall's biscuits are legendary to those who know him well. My family gets panicky at the idea of a holiday or family dinner without these jewels. They're wonderful at morning, noon or night, and he'll often dress them up with minced herbs from our garden. Serve them split in half and draped with a blanket of his dreamy sausage gravy, or spread them with some of my Pear-Cherry Compote, above — or just with good butter. One caveat: Try to handle the dough as little as possible, or you will have tough biscuits.

Yield: 20 small or 10 large biscuits

2 cups unbleached all-purpose flour, plus more for dusting the board
1 tablespoon baking powder
1 teaspoon sea salt
1/4 teaspoon baking soda
6 tablespoons butter, very cold
1 cup buttermilk
1 to 2 teaspoons minced fresh herbs, if desired
2 to 3 tablespoons melted butter
Coarse sea salt for garnish

Preheat oven to 350°. Dust a board or other work surface with flour. Combine dry ingredients in bowl of food processor.

Cut butter into chunks and cut chunks into flour until mixture resembles coarse meal (pulse briefly a few times until this consistency is achieved). Add buttermilk and herbs, if using, and mix just until combined. Dough should be wet; if it appears to be on the dry side, mix in a bit more buttermilk.

Turn dough out onto floured board. Gently pat dough out (do NOT roll with a rolling pin) until it's about 1/2-inch thick. Fold the dough over itself about 5 times, gently pressing dough down to a 1-inch thickness. Cut out biscuits with a round cutter and arrange them on a cookie sheet; if you like soft sides, place them touching each other; for crusty sides, space them an inch apart (these will not rise as high as the more closely spaced biscuits). Incorporate dough scraps together with your hands and pat out again for cutting, until all dough is used. Or use a knife to cut the dough into squares for appetizer biscuits. Brush tops with melted butter and sprinkle with coarse sea salt.

Bake for 10 to 12 minutes; the biscuits should be a beautiful light golden-brown on top and bottom. Do not overbake.

You can make these biscuits, cut them out, arrange them on cookie sheets and freeze; then store the frozen biscuits in a self-sealing freezer bag for up to a month. When you want fresh biscuits, just place the frozen biscuits on a cookie sheet and bake at 450° for about 20 minutes.

SOUTHERN SAUSAGE GRAVY

Yield: 4 cups

1 pound bulk sausage (medium, spicy or sage)
1/4 to 1/2 cup all-purpose flour
4 cups whole milk
Salt and pepper to taste
Crushed red pepper to taste, if desired

In a large, deep skillet over medium to medium-high heat, brown the sausage, breaking it into small pieces as you stir and cook. Remove browned sausage from heat and transfer with a slotted spoon to a medium bowl, reserving drippings in pan. Sprinkle flour over the sausage, tossing with a wooden spoon, using just enough flour to lightly coat all the sausage crumbles. Set aside.

Return skillet with drippings to the burner, on medium to medium-high heat. Gradually stir milk into the drippings. When mixture is thoroughly warm, gradually add the floured sausage to the pan, stirring constantly. As mixture thickens, add salt and pepper to taste. If you like your gravy spicy, add some crushed red pepper. Otherwise, serve with a bottle of Louisiana hot sauce on the side.

FRUIT SALAD WITH LEMON-LAVENDER
SIMPLE SYRUP

Nothing brightens a table more than a bowl of colorful fresh fruit. And when the menu is laden with heavy foods, as this one is, something virtuous is typically appreciated. Go with whatever fruits are freshest and most seasonal, of course. Great fruit doesn't require any enhancements, but this simple syrup is always a hit. You'll have quite a bit of the syrup left over, as this recipe yields about 2 cups, but it keeps well, so you can use it for your next fruit salad, and it makes a lovely replacement for plain simple syrup in many cocktails — you can use a dash of it in your mimosas, too!

Yield: 16 servings

Simple syrup:
2 cups water
1 cup sugar
Juice of 3 lemons
1 tablespoon finely grated lemon zest
1 tablespoon fresh or dried lavender buds

Salad:
3 cups cubed cantaloupe
2 cups strawberries, hulled and sliced
2 cups seedless green and red grapes
2 cups blueberries
2 cups cubed pineapple

Simple syrup: Combine all ingredients in a medium saucepan over medium high heat. Bring to a gentle boil, then reduce heat to low. Continue to simmer and stir for about 5 minutes, until sugar dissolves. Remove from heat and allow to cool. When mixture reaches room temperature, strain and discard solids. Transfer strained syrup to jar with tight-fitting lid. This keeps in the refrigerator for 3 weeks.

Salad: Toss fruit together in a large bowl. Cover and chill until time to serve. Just before serving, drizzle about 1/4 cup syrup over the fruit and toss.

BUTTERY CINNAMON-PECAN MONKEY BREAD

Yes, we're a bit heavy on the breads for this tailgate, but it's brunch! Let's live a little! This monkey bread is irresistible; you'll probably want to make two. Vary the pecans with chopped walnuts and add dried fruits such as raisins, cranberries or sour cherries, if you like.

Yield: 16 servings

3/4 cup butter, melted, divided
1 cup pecan pieces, divided
1/2 cup sugar
1/2 cup brown sugar
2 tablespoons ground cinnamon
3 (7.5-oz.) cans refrigerated biscuits
1 teaspoon pure vanilla extract

Heat oven to 350°. Brush a Bundt pan with 1/4 cup of the melted butter and sprinkle about 1/3 of the pecan pieces in the pan.

Thoroughly combine sugars and cinnamon in a shallow bowl. Cut biscuit dough rounds into four pieces each and roll these in the sugar mixture; reserve remaining sugar mixture. Arrange half the coated biscuit pieces (1 1/2 cans) in the prepared pan — they will be cozily snuggled up to one another — and top with another 1/3 of the pecan pieces. Top with the remaining coated biscuit pieces and finish with the rest of the pecan pieces.

Mix remaining 1/2 cup melted butter with leftover sugar mixture and the vanilla; pour over biscuits in pan. Bake 35 to 45 minutes or until puffed and golden brown. Cool for 5 to 10 minutes; invert on a serving plate.

JANIE'S PERFECT BLOODY MARYS

My mama, Janie Spicer, a native of New Orleans, makes a mean Bloody Mary. Once when she was at a brunch party on Martha's Vineyard, she remarked to the man standing next to her at the bar that she could make a better Bloody Mary than the bartender was doing. The gentleman took her up on her boast and asked the bartender if she could step behind the bar and try her hand. My mother whipped up one of her Bloody Marys and handed it to her fellow guest. He declared it just as good as she'd promised. That gentleman's name was Walter Cronkite, by the way. Here's Janie's Bloody Mary, perfect for a crowd of discerning guests. If you want to add a New Orleans flair, include pickled green beans as a garnish.

Yield: About 20 (6.5-oz.) cocktails

3/4 cup freshly squeezed lime juice (from about 10 limes)
1/3 cup prepared horseradish
3 tablespoons celery seed
12 cups (3 quarts) chilled tomato juice
3 3/4 cups vodka, chilled
1/3 cup Louisiana hot sauce
3 tablespoons Worcestershire sauce
Salt to taste
Trimmed celery stalks with leaves, for garnish, optional
Olives, for garnish, optional
Lime wheels, for garnish, optional
Pickled green beans for garnish, optional

In a large glass, muddle the lime juice, horseradish and celery seed together, mashing celery seeds well. Transfer to drink dispenser. Add tomato juice, vodka, hot sauce, Worcestershire sauce and salt to taste; mix well. Serve in glasses over ice and add any or all of the above suggested garnishes. For those liking extra snap, offer a bottle of Crystal hot sauce alongside.

A MIMOSA BAR

Sparkling wine with splashes of juice is the preferred morning toddy for lots of guests. The traditional mimosa calls for fresh orange juice, of course — but why stop there? Make a mimosa bar for guests to concoct their own libations, with garnishes alongside. Keep the bubbly on ice in a bucket — we typically offer cava or prosecco, the affordable sparkling wines from Spain and Italy, respectively — and provide carafes of juices and bowls of garnish choices. Here are some ideas.

Bubbly: Among cavas, the best-known inexpensive brand is Freixenet Sparkling Cordon Negro Brut, in the black bottle; another good and affordable choice is Segura Viudas Brut Reserva. Prosecco choices include La Marca, with an easily recognized label of robin's egg blue; Ruffino, with a sunny orange label; and Cavit Lunetta, with a crescent moon on its label. All are inexpensive.

Juices: Orange, blood orange and grapefruit are the most popular. Other great choices include cranberry, pomegranate-cherry and pomegranate-blueberry, as well as mango and pineapple. At Central Market, the grocery nearest our house, we find excellent handmade juices like apple-lemon-ginger that would be delightful when spiked with bubbles.

Garnishes: Little bowls filled with fresh mint sprigs, sliced strawberries, raspberries, blueberries, blackberries, orange wheels and pomegranate seeds will pretty up the table.

●●●

Logistics: Wake up early to bake the biscuits and Tater Tot Breakfast Bake (as well as the monkey bread, if you didn't bake it the night before). They all bake at the same temperature, so use both racks of your oven. Once those are in the oven, you can make the gravy.

You may prefer to make and bake the monkey bread the night before; it's fine served at room temperature, and you can transport it in the Bundt pan. Or you can make the recipe up to the point of baking, cover the pan securely with foil or plastic wrap and refrigerate overnight; be sure to bring to room temperature before baking in the morning.

For the biscuits, you can make the dough, cut out the biscuits and arrange them on parchment-paper-lined baking sheets the night before; cover the baking sheets snugly with plastic wrap and store them in the fridge. In the morning, take them out and allow them to sit at room temperature about 20 to 30 minutes before baking. (Or bake them even farther in advance and follow the directions in the recipe for freezing.) We bake the biscuits just before leaving home and keep them warm in the Cambro for the trip. At the tailgate, they go into one of the chafing pans over heat (they are still tasty served at room temp but better if kept warm over Sterno).

For the gravy, transport it in a foil serving pan, covered securely with heavy-duty foil and carried in the Cambro to keep warm. On site, it goes into the wire stands over Sterno heat.

Set up your self-serve granola parfait station in this order: bowls, yogurt, granola, compote and spoons.

Don't forget: Bowls and spoons for the granola; muddler and hot sauce for the Bloody Marys; ice bucket for the sparkling wine and the garnishes for the mimosa bar.

A TACO FIESTA

Picadillo Tacos
Chicken Tinga Tacos
Black Bean Confetti Salad
New Mexico Green Chile con Queso
Top-Shelf Guacamole
Golden Apple-Cranberry Empanadas
Cocktail: Frosty Pineapple Mojitos

When Marshall moved back to Texas after 30-plus years in the frozen north a few years ago, he was astonished by the fascination we have developed with tacos. When he left, "tacos" still meant pre-fried rigid shells filled with ground beef, tomatoes, lettuce and cheese, not the fragrant, supple soft-tortilla variety we have come to embrace. Me, I think tacos are the perfect food, thanks to the wonder that is a tortilla. Within its fold you can put anything, for a tasty, handheld meal, Mexican, Tex-Mex or beyond — we've seen tacos filled with everything from falafel to fried oysters in Texas restaurants.

The right tortilla is important, whether you prefer corn or flour. Most important, that tortilla needs to be fresh, fresh, fresh. In most Texas cities, we are blessed with bakeries and grocery stores and tortillerias making them as you watch. The key to a successful tailgate with this menu is making sure the tortillas feel and taste as fresh as possible. If we're feeling fancy, we'll warm them to order at the tailgate, on a skillet we keep hot on a tabletop gas burner, but usually we just keep them warm in one of our covered disposable chafing dishes.

The trick is to stack the tortillas with sheets of wax paper between them; otherwise they'll stick together. Don't forget garnishes for guests to add to their tacos as they like — shredded cheeses, finely chopped onion, chopped cilantro, shredded cabbage, thinly sliced radishes, thinly sliced raw or pickled jalapeño are among your choices; lime wedges to squeeze over the fillings are essential. The tacos don't need any additional salsas because each has its own sauce, but feel free to set out bowls of your favorite salsas for dipping along with the guacamole and queso.

PICADILLO TACOS

Some people think picadillo *is a just a fancy word for ground beef. But it's more than that: This ground beef bears special seasonings of chile and cinnamon, with additions of raisins and almonds. You find this delicacy all over Mexico, often used as a filling for chiles rellenos, but these flavors speak to Northern Mexico, and to the town where I first tasted this — San Miguel de Allende. The picadillo's nuanced depth of flavor makes this a special taco.*

Yield: 12 servings

1 tablespoon olive oil
1 medium yellow onion, diced
2 cloves garlic, minced
1 1/2 pounds lean ground beef
28-oz. can whole tomatoes
2 teaspoons ground red chile, such as ancho or chipotle
1 teaspoon ground cinnamon
1/4 cup golden raisins

1/4 cup slivered almonds, toasted
Sea salt to taste
12 fresh corn tortillas
2 cups grated sharp cheddar cheese, for serving
Shredded lettuce, for serving
Chopped tomato, for serving
Lime wedges, for squeezing over filling

In a large skillet over medium heat, heat the olive oil and sauté onion
for 5 minutes, until translucent. Add garlic, stir and sauté another
3 minutes. Add ground beef and cook, stirring frequently, until
browned, another 5 to 10 minutes.

In a blender, puree tomatoes with their juices; add to the skillet
along with ground chile, cinnamon and raisins. Simmer, uncovered,
over medium-low heat for about 20 minutes, allowing flavors to
meld. If excess fat has been rendered, spoon or pour it off at this
point; then continue to cook down until liquids have reduced, per-
haps another 10 minutes. Stir in almonds, taste and add sea salt if
needed.

Serve in warmed tortillas with cheese, lettuce and tomato, if desired,
and a squeeze of lime, if you like.

CHICKEN TINGA TACOS

*Until I tasted tinga, I found shredded-chicken tacos a tad boring. This
recipe changes all such perceptions with a balance of tomato, chile,
herbs and seasonings. The smokiness of the chipotles (canned chiles
in adobo are widely available in supermarkets, at least in Texas)*

and the addition of a hint of cinnamon and green olives (use quality olives, please!) set this taco apart. Find queso fresco in Mexican grocery stores and a few gourmet stores, too. Otherwise, shredded jack cheese is fine.

Yield: 12 servings

8 to 10 boneless, skinless chicken thighs
Salt and pepper, to taste
1 tablespoon olive oil
1 medium yellow onion, sliced thin
28-oz. can whole tomatoes
1/2 cup chopped green olives
2 canned chipotle chiles, seeded, minced
1 tablespoon adobo sauce from chipotles
1 teaspoon dried Mexican oregano
1 teaspoon ground cumin
1/4 teaspoon ground cinnamon
Sea salt to taste
12 corn or flour tortillas
1 cup crumbled queso fresco or jack cheese
Shredded green and purple cabbage, for serving
Lime wedges, for squeezing

Heat oven to 350°. Season chicken thighs with salt and pepper and arrange in a large (11-by-9-inch) casserole dish; roast for 45 minutes, or until juices run clear. Let chicken cool until it can be handled; then shred chicken meat and transfer to a large bowl.

Meanwhile, heat olive oil in a large sauté pan over medium heat and sauté onion, stirring frequently, until translucent.

In a blender, puree tomatoes with juices in a blender and add to onion in pan. Stir in olives, minced chipotles and adobo sauce, oregano, cumin, cinnamon and salt to taste. Simmer uncovered for 30 minutes, allowing flavors to meld and mixture to reduce and thicken. Combine sauce with shredded chicken. Serve in warm tortillas with cheese, shredded cabbage and squeezes of fresh lime.

NEW MEXICO GREEN CHILE CON QUESO

If you go to Mexico and order "queso," you'll get a blank look. That just means cheese — any and all cheese. In Texas, we've shortened chile con queso, *the proper name for the chile-cheese dip, to* queso. *It's such a ubiquitous snack, with such versatility, that my friend and colleague Lisa Fain, who writes the popular blog Homesick Texan, penned an entire cookbook called "Queso!" I've borrowed ideas from a few different recipes of hers to put together the sort of queso I like making most at home. It employs the much-maligned but easy-melting Velveeta, punched up with an equal amount of sharp white cheddar. New Mexico green chiles (see note) add an earthy, smoky fragrance that the wan canned varieties can't match. Personally, I like a lot of green chile, but this recipe keeps it in moderation. My special ingredient is refried beans, to add depth and body.*

Yield: 12 servings

1 tablespoon butter
2/3 cup chopped sweet yellow onion
2 cloves garlic, minced
2 jalapeños, seeded and minced
3 tablespoons chili powder

3 teaspoons ground cumin
1/2 pound processed American cheese, such as Velveeta, cubed
1/2 pound sharp white cheddar, cubed
1 cup canned refried beans
2 New Mexico green chiles, roasted, with peel, stem and seeds
   removed, then chopped (see note)
2 to 3 tablespoons half-and-half
Sea salt to taste

In a large saucepan, heat the butter over medium-high heat and
sauté onion until translucent, about 5 minutes. Add garlic and
jalapeños and sauté, stirring, until vegetables are softened. Stir in
chili powder and cumin until blended. Add cubed cheeses and stir
as cheese melts. Reduce heat to medium low and stir in refried
beans and roasted green chiles. If mixture is too thick and clumpy,
stir in enough half-and-half, a tablespoon or so at a time, to keep it
smooth. Add salt to taste (you may not need it, as both the cheeses
and the beans have salt). Serve warm with crisp tortilla chips.

NOTE: Luckily, green-chile season roughly coincides with the start
of tailgate season, beginning in August and extending into early fall.
During that time, many Texas markets offer New Mexico green chiles
(often labeled Hatch green chiles) fresh or already roasted; stock up
while you can, as the roasted chiles freeze well. Some markets also
stock frozen roasted green chiles year-round, and they are readily
available for shipping online. To roast fresh green chiles: Place them
on a baking sheet, brushing with 1 teaspoon olive oil each, and roast
in a 400° oven for 35 to 40 minutes, or until charred on all sides.
When they're cool enough to handle, peel off the charred skins and
discard, along with the stems and seeds, before chopping the chiles.

BLACK BEAN CONFETTI SALAD

The genius of this salad is that it doubles as a side dish and as a taco filling for your vegetarian guests. If you've mastered the Instant Pot and want to make black beans from scratch, please do — we're fans of the process. But if you're really short on time, there's no shame whatsoever in using canned — just be sure you rinse and drain them well. If fresh corn is in season, you should absolutely use it, but frozen and thawed is dandy if fresh corn isn't available; as for the apples, I like Granny Smith or similar tart varieties for the perky boost they give to this salad. If you're making and serving it right away, there's no worry about the apples turning brown. Otherwise, be sure to toss the apple dice in some lemon juice immediately after you cut them up. Finally, you can use typical chili powder here, but we recommend ground red chiles such as those found at Pendery's, penderys.com.

Yield: 12 servings

Salad:
2 (15-oz.) cans black beans, rinsed and drained
2 cups fresh corn cut from the cob, or frozen, defrosted and drained
2 cups diced red bell pepper
2 bunches green onion, white and green parts, diced
2 Granny Smith apples, cored and diced
3/4 cups fresh cilantro leaves, coarsely chopped
Juice of 2 limes

Dressing:
2 tablespoons extra-virgin olive oil
1 teaspoon sea salt
1 teaspoon ground cumin
1 teaspoon ground red chiles

Salad: In a large bowl, combine beans, corn, red bell pepper, green onion, apples, cilantro and lime juice. Toss well.

Dressing: Place all ingredients in the container you'll be using to transport the dressing. Shake to mix well.

Assembly: On site, shake dressing well and drizzle over salad, tossing well. Cover salad and allow flavors to meld for 30 minutes. Serve cool or at room temperature.

TOP-SHELF GUACAMOLE

Nothing is easier or more delicious than freshly made guacamole. Don't fall for the prefab version at the grocery that comes in the vacuum-sealed packages and is pumped full of preservatives — though many grocery stores make guac fresh daily, and it's usually good, if expensive. Find perfectly ripe avocados, however, and this is the best you can make. Serve with crisp tortilla chips; our favorite brands are Juanita's, Santitas, Julio's, Mission, Xochitl and El Milagro. Feel free to offer your favorite salsa on the side for dipping as well, if you like.

Yield: 12 servings

4 large ripe avocados
2 Roma tomatoes, finely diced
3/4 cup diced sweet yellow onion
1 jalapeño, seeded and minced
1 tablespoon minced cilantro leaves
Juice of 2 lemons or 3 limes
1 to 2 teaspoons ground cumin, to taste

Sea salt to taste

Mash the avocados with a fork until smooth in a large bowl. Still using the fork, stir in tomato, onion, jalapeño, cilantro and citrus juice; blending until the mixture is smooth. Stir in cumin (start with 1 teaspoon — cumin is a strong spice and can easily overwhelm a dish) and salt to taste. Serve with crisp tortilla chips.

GOLDEN APPLE-CRANBERRY EMPANADAS

While much of our Mexican-food-loving population clamors for tres leches cake, flan or churros for a sweet, I'm a fool for empanadas. These are little hand pies or turnovers, filled with fruit. The majority found in Mexican bakeries have pumpkin or sweet-potato or pineapple filling, but I think the apple-cranberry combination is too good to resist. If you have a homemade pie crust recipe you love, make it. Otherwise, ready-made crust from the grocery store's refrigerator section is just fine.

Yield: 16 empanadas

2 boxes ready-made pie crusts (for a total of 4 crusts)
4 cups peeled, chopped apples
1 cup dried cranberries
1/2 cup sugar
1/2 cup apple juice
2 teaspoons ground cinnamon
All-purpose flour, for dusting work surface
1 egg, beaten
1 tablespoon water

Coarse sugar crystals (see note) for garnish

Unroll pie crusts and allow to sit at room temperature for 20 minutes (or according to package instructions). If making your own dough, divide the dough into 16 equal-size pieces and form them into balls or discs; place on a baking sheet, cover with a dishtowel and place in the fridge while you make the filling.

For the filling, in a large saucepan, combine apples, cranberries, sugar, apple juice and cinnamon, stirring well over medium-high heat, until the mixture just comes to a boil. Reduce heat to low and allow to simmer, uncovered, for 10 minutes. Remove from heat and allow to cool.

While filling is cooling, preheat oven to 400°. On work surface dusted with flour, cut each purchased crust into fourths, or roll out your from-scratch dough into 16 circles about 1/4-inch thick.

To assemble pies, spoon about 1/2 cup of the fruit mixture onto each wedge of pie crust (or each round, for from-scratch) and fold crust over to cover the filling. (The homemade dough will produce the traditional crescent shape; the quarters of purchased dough make more triangular pies.) Using fork tines, crimp and seal the edges of the crust together to make a pastry package.

Place filled crusts on ungreased baking sheets and make three tiny slits with a sharp paring knife in each crust to vent steam. Mix beaten egg with water to make an egg wash; brush the wash over each empanada. Bake 18 to 20 minutes, or until golden brown. Sprinkle with coarse sugar while still warm. Serve warm or at room temperature.

NOTE: Icing, sanding, decorating and turbinado sugars have coarser crystals than regular granulated sugar. The baking aisle of your supermarket should have at least one of them.

FROSTY PINEAPPLE MOJITOS

Since mojitos have become a rage in the U.S., it's hard to remember that they're not Mexican in origin; they're actually from Cuba. No matter. The flavor profile of rum and lime and mint works perfectly with our menu, and we've added pineapple for extra oomph. If you really want to make this with tequila instead of rum, go for it! If you insist on margaritas, see the Mango-Mint Margaritas recipe in the "Chilly Saturday" chapter, Page 110.

Yield: 24 (6-oz.) cocktails

4 cups fresh mint leaves, divided
1 liter chilled white rum
4 cups chilled pineapple juice
3 cups chilled fresh lime juice
4 cups fresh mint leaves, divided
4 cups cubed pineapple, frozen
2 (1-liter) chilled bottles sparkling water, plain or lime
Extra mint sprigs for garnish

In a pitcher, muddle 2 cups of the mint with a few splashes of rum — just enough to release the essence of the herbs. Don't bludgeon the leaves! Transfer to the drink dispenser. Add all the rum, pineapple juice and lime juice, plus the remaining 2 cups mint. Just before serving, add frozen pineapple to the dispenser. To serve, pour mixture over ice in a glass, leaving room at the top to add a splash of sparkling water. Stir and garnish with mint sprig.

•••

Logistics: Pack the tortillas with waxed paper between them to keep them from sticking together. At the site, keep warm in a covered foil pan over Sterno heat, making sure to keep tortillas separated individually with the waxed-paper sheets.

Start your self-serve line with the tortillas; then fillings, kept warm in pans over Sterno heat; followed by queso, also kept warm in a foil pan over Sterno. Then come the bowls of garnishes; then the black bean salad and guacamole and then the dessert empanadas. Position bowls of tortilla chips as near the queso and the guacamole as possible.

For the salad, pack the dressing separately in a jar with tight-fitting lid; at the tailgate, dress and toss the salad just before serving.

Tortilla chips become stale quickly once exposed to air and humidity, so don't dump all your bags in a big bowl at once to serve. Open only one bag at a time and keep an eye on the chip bowls so you can replenish as needed from your stash of sealed bags.

Don't forget: Tortilla chips for the guacamole and queso — figure on at least a couple of the larger (11- or 12-oz.) bags — and garnishes for the tacos. Muddler for the cocktail and mint sprigs for the garnish. This menu has a lot of moving parts, so pay close attention to your checklist to make sure nothing's left behind.

PORK & BEANS & MORE

Coffee-Rubbed Smoked Pork Tenderloin Sliders
Grilled Sweet-Corn Salad
Sweet and Smoky Baked Beans With Smokehouse
  Sausage
Nutella Snickerdoodle Sandwich Cookies
Cocktail: Grapefruit Junebug

One of our best investments over the past few years has been our smoker, the Big Green Egg knockoff that we affectionately call our Big Fake Egg. The kamado-style smoker-grill design (so named for its Japanese origin) facilitates efficient cooking; it's quick and fool-proof — if you follow the instructions and watch your temperature and time. A meat thermometer with a remote monitor frees us to work on other food in the house while the smoker is doing its thing outside. Our Big Fake Egg is especially handy when we need to feed a crowd, and there's seemingly no end to the list of meats that are so much better with woodsmoke flavor (Marshall's smoked prime rib at Christmas is unbelievable). Pork tenderloin is especially easy; it cooks in no time and is perfect for serving on silver-dollar-size rolls. Sliders are the ideal tailgate food, as they're handheld. Kids love them too. To go alongside, my Sweet and Smoky Beans and Grilled Sweet-Corn Salad are both crowd-pleasers.

COFFEE-RUBBED SMOKED PORK TENDERLOIN SLIDERS

Brining is so important for keeping the pork juicy. If you don't have a smoker, you can sear the rubbed tenderloins in a cast-iron skillet over the stove and finish them in a 450° oven for about 5 minutes — the rub assures that they'll be delicious even without the woodsmoke flavor that sends them over the top. It's an irresistible blend of ground coffee, dark-brown sugar, salt and ground red chile that caramelizes on the meat. The recipe below yields about 4 1/2 cups; you can refrigerate what's left over in an airtight container for up to a month and use it on chicken or steak, ribs or burgers. This pork makes a handsome centerpiece for a more formal meal, but for our tailgates we slice it about 1/4- to 1/2-inch thick and serve it with silver-dollar rolls or other small round dinner rolls. I like these sandwiches with a spicy brown mustard, or with mayonnaise spiked with hot sauce, or with one of our barbecue sauces on pages 26 and 38.

Yield: 12 servings

Brine:
2 quarts water
1/2 cup sea salt
1/2 cup brown sugar
2 teaspoons granulated garlic
1 teaspoon dried Mexican oregano

Pork:
3 (1-pound) pork tenderloins, trimmed

Coffee-chile rub:
2 cups ground dark-roast coffee beans
2 cups dark-brown sugar

3 tablespoons sea salt
1 to 2 tablespoons ground red chiles

To smoke:
Olive oil for brushing

Brine: Bring water, salt, brown sugar, garlic and Mexican oregano to a boil in a medium pan over medium-high heat. Reduce heat to low and simmer until salt and sugar dissolve. Allow to cool while you proceed with the pork.

Pork: Using a sharp boning knife, trim silverskin and any sinew from tenderloin. Place in a large glass or plastic container. When brine has cooled enough that its heat won't cook the pork, pour brine over pork and refrigerate overnight.

Rub: Combine all ingredients in a large bowl and mix well.

To smoke: When ready to smoke, remove pork from brine, pat dry and set aside to come to room temperature.

Set your smoker for direct heat and bring to 450°. Brush the pork with olive oil and cover with rub.

Place tenderloins in smoker and close the lid. Cook on the grill, turning every 5 minutes, until the internal temperature reaches 145°; this typically takes about 25 to 30 minutes — but watch the temperature carefully; you don't want to overcook the tenderloin. Remove the meat to a cutting board and let rest for at least 10 minutes before slicing. (We wrap the whole tenderloins in heavy foil and transport in the Cambro to our tailgate, then slice on-site just before serving time.) For sliders, serve slices between silver-dollar rolls sliced horizontally.

GRILLED SWEET-CORN SALAD

Is there anything better than sweet grilled fresh corn? This one's great in the early football season, which still feels like summer around here. The chili powder adds a subtle Southwestern bottom note. Pack the dressing in a tightly sealed jar and shake vigorously before drizzling on the salad at party time.

Yield: 12 servings

8 ears fresh corn
1/2 cup plus 1 tablespoon olive oil, divided
Salt and pepper to taste
1 pint cherry or grape tomatoes, halved
2 ripe avocados
1/2 cup chopped cilantro leaves
1/4 cup fresh lemon juice
2 tablespoons sherry vinegar
3 teaspoons granulated garlic
2 teaspoons chili powder

Set grill to medium heat. Shuck corn, removing silks; wash and pat dry. Use the 1 tablespoon olive oil to lightly brush all the ears and place the corn on the hot grill. Close grill cover and cook for 15 minutes, turning every 5 minutes, until evenly cooked. Remove corn from grill, season with salt and pepper to taste and set aside to cool.

Slice kernels from cobs with a sharp knife into a large bowl. Add halved tomatoes to the corn. Pit the avocado and dice the flesh; add to bowl. Gently stir in chopped cilantro.

If serving right away, whisk together remaining 1/2 cup olive oil with lemon juice, sherry vinegar, garlic and chili powder and drizzle over salad, tossing to combine. If serving later, combine dressing ingredients in a lidded jar or squeeze bottle. Cover salad directly with plastic wrap, pressing down gently to make sure the plastic is adhering to surface of the salad to help keep avocados from turning brown. Just before serving, vigorously shake dressing to blend and drizzle over salad.

SWEET AND SMOKY BEANS WITH SMOKEHOUSE SAUSAGE

We have available in Texas such great local makers of smoked sausage, such as Pederson's, Opa's and Slovacek's, who follow the smokehouse traditions of the Czech and German people who settled much of Central Texas. We prefer these to the usual grocery-store supply of smoked sausage, which are often loaded with nitrites that impart too much artificial flavor. If you can't get a good local sausage, substitute bacon or a smoked country ham such as Smithfield. If your guests include vegetarians, you can skip the smoked meat altogether, of course, but you could bump up the amount of smoked paprika a bit to compensate for the loss of that smokiness. If you're skipping the meat, use a small amount of olive oil to sauté the onion.

Yield: 12 servings

2 pounds dried navy or Great Northern beans
1 pound smoked sausage, diced
1 yellow onion, diced
4 cups vegetable broth
28-oz. can crushed tomatoes

1/2 cup dark molasses
2 tablespoons granulated garlic
2 tablespoons Pickapeppa sauce
1 tablespoon sweet paprika
1/2 tablespoon smoked paprika
Sea salt and black pepper to taste

If using an Instant Pot (I don't know how we lived without ours), cook beans with remaining ingredients according to Instant Pot directions.

Otherwise, cover beans in water, soak beans overnight and drain before cooking.

In a large Dutch oven, cook sausage and onion together until onions are translucent, about 5 minutes. Add vegetable broth, crushed tomatoes with their juice, molasses, garlic, Pickapeppa and both paprikas, stirring well. Add drained beans and bring to a boil, stir and reduce heat to low, cover and simmer for 2 hours or until done. Add sea salt and pepper to taste.

NUTELLA SNICKERDOODLE SANDWICH COOKIES

Among Marshall's holiday traditions is baking oversized Snicker-doodle cookies for family and friends. We've taken his recipe and downsized the cookies, making them perfect for turning into cookie sandwiches. The pairing of cinnamon-sugar cookies with hazelnut-chocolate spread is sinfully good.

Yield: 24 sandwich cookies

5 1/2 cups flour
4 teaspoons cream of tartar
2 teaspoons baking soda
1 teaspoon salt
2 cups shortening or butter, softened
3 3/4 cups sugar, divided
4 eggs
2 tablespoons cinnamon
3/4 cup Nutella

In a large bowl, whisk together flour, cream of tartar, baking soda and salt; set aside.

In a large mixing bowl, use electric mixer to cream together butter or shortening with 3 cups of the sugar. Add eggs one at a time, mixing well after each addition. Gradually sprinkle in the flour mixture until incorporated. Chill dough for 30 minutes.

While dough is chilling, mix remaining 3/4 cup sugar with cinnamon in a wide, shallow bowl.

When dough is chilled, heat oven to 400° and line 2 cookie sheets with parchment paper. With a melon baller, scoop enough dough to roll between your hands into a ball the size of a jawbreaker; roll the dough ball in the cinnamon-sugar mixture. Repeat until you've made 48 dough balls, spacing them evenly on cookie sheets. Bake for 8 to 10 minutes. Let cookies cool completely on cookie sheets before making the sandwiches.

Make each sandwich by spreading a little Nutella on a cookie and centering another cookie on top.

GRAPEFRUIT JUNEBUG

Some hot summer several years ago, I began making a variety of cocktails with icy-cold vodka and fresh fruit (often berries) muddled with fresh herbs from the kitchen garden (usually basil or mint). I'd top that with sparkling water for the most refreshing hot-weather libation ever. My sister Jennifer dubbed it the Junebug after my childhood nickname. This version combines three of my favorite ingredients ever, grapefruit, mint and super-sparkly Topo Chico, the Mexican mineral water we buy by the case.

Yield: 24 (6-oz.) cocktails

1 liter chilled vodka
1 large bunch mint leaves, pulled from stems
52-oz. chilled bottle pure grapefruit juice, such as Simply Grapefruit
1.5-liter chilled bottle Topo Chico
Ice cubes
Fresh mint sprigs for garnish
Fresh grapefruit wheels, cut into fourths, for garnish

Pour about 1/4 cup vodka into a pitcher with the mint leaves and a shot of grapefruit juice. Muddle just enough to release the mint essence without completely crushing the leaves. Transfer to your drink dispenser. Add all the rest of the vodka and grapefruit juice and stir to mix. At serving time, pour in chilled Topo Chico. Serve in glasses over ice with mint sprig and grapefruit garnish.

•••

Logistics: To transport the pork tenderloins, wrap tightly in heavy foil and keep warm in Cambro on the way to the tailgate. Slice pork on-site, along with slider buns. Keep sliced pork warm over Sterno in foil pans; ditto for slider buns, if you're serving these warm. To ensure maximum freshness for the salad, grill the corn the morning of the tailgate and either mix the salad just before leaving home or pack the ingredients separately in plastic bags and toss the salad together at the tailgate site (to minimize browning of avocados, you could bring the whole avocados to the site, dice them there and add them just before serving).

Don't forget: Rolls and your choice of condiments for the sliders, garnishes for Junebugs. Bring a cutting board and sharp knife to slice tenderloins and slider buns on-site.

BRATS!

Grilled Bratwurst and Onions With Sauerkraut
Oktoberfest Braised Red Cabbage and Apples
German Potato Salad
Cast-Iron Skillet Apple Upside-Down Cake
Cocktail: The Shandy Bar

None of our family is from Wisconsin. In fact, we're Texans through and through. But we understand that you cannot have a proper tailgate season without putting bratwurst on the menu at least once. Marshall's folks, Marshall and Marlene Harris, have a good friend in Hal Lambert, who played football at TCU with the elder Marshall in the early 1950s. Hal will show up at the tailgate and holler, "Where are the brats?" to remind us he really likes brats better than anything else we serve. We make our brat party a celebration rich in German traditions (which abound in Texas), with sauerkraut, braised red cabbage and German potato salad. You can make your shandy — a combination of lemonade and beer — especially German, too, by choosing Beck's, Bitburger, König Pilsener, Paulaner or another beer from Germany (and there are plenty of wonderful German-style beers made right here in the USA). If guests need snacks while you're getting the grill going, lay out a platter of Black Forest ham slices, beer sausage, emmentaler cheese, sliced apples, grapes, pretzels and a hearty German-style mustard.

GRILLED BRATWURST AND ONIONS WITH SAUERKRAUT

If you have a good butcher shop nearby, chances are you can find authentic bratwurst and knackwurst. If not, the grocery store varieties are OK. Be sure to lay in a good selection of mustards (brown, spicy brown, grainy, Dijon, etc.) and good-quality sauerkraut — the current foodie fascination with fermentation means you might even be able to find locally made kraut from an artisanal pickler. We pack a jar of the chow-chow Marshall makes from our garden produce; you can find good commercial chow-chows or similar relishes — including Fort Worth's Mrs. Renfro's, which is sold across the nation — in the grocery store. If you have a good German deli around, buy the brat buns there. Otherwise, hoagie rolls are great. We like to pile the plump grilled sausages atop the grilled onions on a big platter and surround them with sauerkraut.

Yield: 12 to 14 servings

1/2 cup olive oil
3 large red onions, trimmed and sliced about 1/2-inch thick
Sea salt to taste
5 pounds bratwurst (about 25 sausages)
28-oz. jar good-quality sauerkraut, drained

Prepare grill to medium heat and brush grates with some of the olive oil. Brush onion slices with remaining oil and sprinkle with sea salt to taste. Grill onions on each side until tender, about 6 or 7 minutes total. Transfer to a large serving platter.

Lower grill to medium-low heat and grill brats, turning occasionally, until meat thermometer inserted at center of a sausage reaches

165°, about 10 to 15 minutes. Transfer brats to platter atop onions.

Arrange sauerkraut around the perimeter of the platter.

Serve with buns (lightly toasted on the grill, if you have time) and an assortment of mustards and relishes.

OKTOBERFEST BRAISED RED CABBAGE AND APPLES

Even people who don't think they like cabbage love this. The addition of apples, along with the sweet-and-sour play of the vinegar and brown sugar, makes it a dish with unexpected verve and beautiful color. We like it also with smoked pork tenderloin or pork chops.

Yield: 12 to 14 servings

1/4 cup butter
3 red apples, cored and sliced thick
3 red cabbages, cored and sliced into thick shreds
1/4 cup apple-cider vinegar
1 tablespoon brown sugar
3/4 cup water
Sea salt and black pepper to taste

In a large Dutch oven, melt butter over medium heat. Add apple slices and stir, sautéing for about 5 to 8 minutes. Add cabbage, vinegar and brown sugar, stirring well. Add water and bring to a gentle boil, then reduce heat to low and simmer, covered, for 30 minutes or till cabbage is wilted and just tender. Adjust seasonings with salt and pepper to taste. Serve warm at the tailgate in foil pan over Sterno.

GERMAN POTATO SALAD

The great potato-salad divide in Texas is between mayonnaise-based potato salad, which is chilled before serving, and German potato salad, flavored with mustard and bacon and typically served warm (although nobody complains when we serve it at room temp at our tailgates). This wonderful potato salad was one of my dad's specialties, and I can happily eat it for a meal, all by itself. If you want to make a vegetarian version, leave out the bacon and simply sauté the onion in a little olive oil. If the potatoes are small, cut them in half; if large, into fourths.

Yield: 12 to 14 servings

4 pounds new potatoes, scrubbed and cut in half or quartered
1 tablespoon plus 2 teaspoons sea salt, divided
1 pound thick-sliced bacon, diced
1 yellow onion, diced
1 cup vegetable broth
2/3 cup apple-cider vinegar
3 tablespoons whole-grain mustard
1 tablespoon sugar
Black pepper to taste
1 bunch green onions, green and white parts, chopped

Place potatoes in a large pot of cold water and add 1 tablespoon of the salt. Cover, bring water to a boil and reduce to a steady simmer, cooking potatoes until easily pierced with a fork, about 10 minutes. Drain and set aside.

While potatoes are cooking, scatter bacon dice in a heavy skillet and heat over medium heat. Cook, stirring frequently and lowering heat if needed to keep bacon from burning, until bacon is browned and almost crisp; transfer bacon to paper towels to drain but leave drippings in skillet.

Add onion to skillet and cook over medium heat, stirring frequently, until translucent, about 5 minutes. Stir in vegetable broth, vinegar, mustard and sugar, scraping skillet for any brown bits, and cook, stirring occasionally, for 15 minutes or until mixture has thickened and reduced by half. Add cooked potatoes to the skillet and stir well. Add drained bacon and mix to combine. Turn heat to low, season with remaining salt and black pepper to taste, and cook for another 5 minutes to allow flavors to meld. Transfer to a bowl and serve topped with chopped green onions.

CAST-IRON SKILLET APPLE UPSIDE-DOWN CAKE

Next to a good knife, the cast-iron skillet is my favorite kitchen tool. It's the perfect vehicle for any kind of upside-down cake. You can serve whipped cream on top, spiced up with a little cinnamon.

Yield: 10 to 12 servings

Caramel and apples:
1/4 cup butter
2/3 cup lightly packed dark-brown sugar
1 teaspoon pure vanilla extract, divided
1 teaspoon ground cinnamon, divided
1/2 teaspoon ground nutmeg
Pinch sea salt
3/4 cup golden raisins

1/2 cup sliced almonds

2 red delicious apples, peeled, cored and cut into 1/2-inch-thick
slices

Cake:

1 3/4 cup all-purpose flour

3/4 teaspoon baking powder

1 teaspoon ground cinnamon

1 teaspoon sea salt

1/2 cup butter, melted

1 cup granulated sugar

1/2 cup lightly packed dark-brown sugar

2 large eggs

1 teaspoon vanilla

3/4 cup apple juice

Whipped cream and cinnamon for serving, if desired

Caramel and apples: In a 10-inch cast-iron skillet over medium heat,
combine butter with brown sugar, vanilla, cinnamon, nutmeg and
pinch of salt. Stir well and continue to simmer until thickened and
a light caramel in color. Remove from heat and scatter raisins and
almonds evenly atop the caramel mixture, then arrange apple slices
in a circular pattern in one layer on top. Set aside.

Cake: Heat oven to 350°.

In a large bowl, whisk together flour, baking powder, cinnamon and
salt.

In a second large bowl, blend together butter, granulated sugar and
brown sugar, mixing well. Add eggs one at a time, blending just till
combined. Stir in vanilla.

Gradually stir dry ingredients into wet ones. Add apple juice and mix just until incorporated.

Carefully pour batter over apple-caramel mixture in cast-iron pan and bake 1 hour, or until toothpick inserted at center comes away clean. Allow cake to cool 15 to 20 minutes in the pan before inverting onto serving plate. Cool completely before slicing to serve. If you like, top with whipped cream sprinkled with a little cinnamon.

THE SHANDY BAR

A good warm-weather sipper, the shandy has either British or German roots, depending on which history you believe. The name "shandy" derives from the British "shandygaff," which referred to a half-and-half combination of pilsner and ginger beer that dates from the 1800s. In Germany, the beer-and-lemon-soda drink is called the "radler," which means "cyclist," and most stories attribute it to a tavernkeeper who cut his beer with lemon soda for thirsty cyclists. The modern shandy is most typically served as a beer-and-lemonade blend. We think a shandy can be made with any sort of fruit juice, and it's especially enjoyable with some extra sparkle. You don't have to stick to lagers, but you do want to avoid darker or heavier beers for shandys.

Set up the Shandy Bar much as you would the Mimosa Bar on Page 59, offering some variation on these beer and juice options:

Beers

• Sour or tart German-style beer.

- Berliner weisse-style or wheat beer.

- Belgian ale.

- IPA.

Juices

- Freshly squeezed orange, grapefruit or blood-orange juice.

- Watermelon juice (simply puree watermelon chunks in a blender).

- Strawberry lemonade.

Sparklers

- Top any of these with grapefruit-, orange- or lemon-flavored sparkling water.

For those preferring wine over beer, you can swap in a dry riesling for the beer element — but make sure the riesling is a very dry one or your sipper will be far too sweet. Dry ciders, available in greater and greater variety, could also be fun to experiment with. The easiest garnishes are quarter-slices of orange and half-slices of lemon.

●●●

Logistics: You can slice the onions in advance and pack them in a self-seal plastic bag. We make the potato salad the morning of the tailgate and serve it at room temperate for simplicity's sake, but you could make it the day before and take it out of the fridge in the morning — it's fine at room temp, but you don't want to serve it chilled.

Don't forget: This is one of the few menus for which we cook on-site, so don't forget to pack the tabletop grill, grill tools and a big platter for serving. Make sure you include the buns and the condiments, too. Since you'll be transporting the cake in the skillet, don't forget the serving plate for it. If you're topping the cake with whipped cream, make sure to pack the freshly whipped cream and the cinnamon, plus a whisk to give it a last-minute whip before serving.

FESTA ITALIANA

Grilled Spiedies
Caprese Salad on Skewers
Tuscan Bean Salad
Sweet-and-Sour Italian Slaw
Lavender Lemon Bars
Cocktail: The Tipsy Gypsy

Though Texas lacks a strong depth of Italian heritage, that doesn't keep Italian cuisine from being a universal favorite, and Marshall and I love to cook it at home. Marshall's years of living in the north — mostly in Ohio and Massachusetts — meant he was surrounded by excellent Italian food much of the time. He brought his recipe for his beloved spiedies home with him, and I've added my Italian spins on slaw and bean salad, as well as the cocktail. The skewered caprese salad is as colorful as it is delicious, and it makes an easy tailgate, picnic or cocktail party nibble. Along with our Chilly Saturday menu in the following chapter, this is one of our most popular tailgates of the season, so our recipes are sized to serve a crowd.

GRILLED SPIEDIES

This is a Marshall K. Harris specialty of the first order. Here's how he describes his longtime relationship with this distinctive specialty sandwich:

"I was first introduced to spiedies (called 'the best sandwich you've never heard of' by Bon Appétit magazine in 2017) when I lived up north in the 1980s. I was visiting family living in Binghamton, N.Y., who took me off to a corner deli when I admitted I'd not heard of spiedies. There I was introduced to this delicious delicacy, as well as to the proper way to eat them. They are as simple as they are satisfying: You take a skewer of grilled marinated meat in one hand and a slice of fresh Italian bread in the other and use the bread to remove the meat from the skewer. The only addition required is maybe some additional spiedie sauce. One never asks for condiments, such ketchup or mustard, if one wishes not to be labeled a heretic. But if you're really hungry, you can have your spiedie meat piled high in a fresh hoagie roll — again, sans any fanciness like peppers and onions, if you want to be authentic. I suppose if you are serving them outside of Binghamton, you can add what you wish, but these morsels of marinated yumminess really require nothing else."

Be sure to have on hand either 8-inch metal skewers or 8-inch wooden skewers that you've soaked in water for 30 minutes just before grilling. The marinade doubles as the dressing that's drizzled on at serving time, so you'll need to reserve half of it for later before you marinate the meat — reusing anything that's been exposed to raw meat is a food-safety no-no.

Yield: 20 servings

5 pounds cubed meat (chicken thighs and/or breasts, or beef sirloin, lamb loin or pork loin, or a combination, cut into 1-inch pieces)
4 cups olive oil
1 cup red-wine vinegar
1 cup fresh lemon juice

1 cup chopped Italian parsley
1 cup chopped mint leaves
6 bay leaves
12 cloves garlic, minced
1/2 cup minced yellow onion
8 teaspoons dried oregano
8 teaspoons black pepper
8 teaspoons sea salt
4 teaspoons dried thyme
4 teaspoons paprika
2 teaspoons dried basil
Pinch dried rosemary
2 loaves Italian bread, sliced

Place meat in a large sealable container.

In a very large bowl or pitcher, mix together all remaining ingredients except for the bread. Stir well, then reserve half the mixture for serving, storing it in a covered container in the refrigerator. Pour the remaining marinade over the meat and marinate overnight, covered, in the refrigerator.

When you're ready to cook, prepare grill to medium-hot and drain marinade from the meat, discarding the marinade. Skewer 4 to 5 pieces of meat on each skewer and grill just 3 to 4 minutes in all, turning once, until evenly browned but still juicy inside. To serve, wrap a slice of bread around the skewer and pull the meat off the stick, enfolding the meat in the bread to make a sandwich. Drizzle with additional sauce, if desired, and enjoy.

CAPRESE SALAD ON SKEWERS

The first time I saw this version of the popular caprese salad at a restaurant, there was a teenager in my dining party, and this approach to salad thoroughly delighted her. These salads-on-a-skewer are not only cute and fun but also an especially neat and easy way to serve the mozzarella-basil-tomato components in a picnic setting, and they're easily transported, too. But note that the quality of the ingredients is of particular importance; seek out the freshest mozzarella (see note) and basil, making sure the basil leaves are vibrant and unblemished. You can use shorter skewers designed for appetizers (I like the thin bamboo variety, found at World Market and at Asian markets) rather than the longer versions. Bring the balsamic vinaigrette in a squeeze bottle to drizzle on at serving time. It's best to put these together the morning of tailgate day, as close to tailgate time as possible.

Yield: 24 servings

48 grape or cherry tomatoes
48 small fresh mozzarella balls (see note)
48 basil leaves
4 tablespoons balsamic vinegar
3 tablespoons extra-virgin olive oil
2 teaspoons Dijon mustard
Sea salt and black pepper to taste

Onto each of 24 skewers, thread tomatoes, mozzarella balls and basil leaves, alternating them so that each skewer has 2 of each. Store skewers in an airtight container in fridge till serving time.

In a plastic squirt bottle, combine vinegar, oil, Dijon and salt and pepper. Shake well and let flavors meld in the fridge for an hour or so. Shake again before drizzling on skewers at serving time.

NOTE: Be sure to look for small mozzarella balls, not the bigger ones; you can find them packed in liquid and refrigerated in some supermarkets, and Italian delis or specialty shops are usually a reliable source. If you can find only the larger ones, you can cut them in half for the skewers, though they won't be as cute. Make sure they are freshly made; buy them no earlier than the day before the tailgate and get them into your fridge as quickly as possible — their delicate milky freshness wanes quickly.

TUSCAN BEAN SALAD

A bean salad this good can be a meal in itself, but it's also the perfect complement to the grilled spiedies. The white balsamic vinegar is a hidden key; in play with the Dijon and fresh herbs, it gives a lot of layered flavor that's really satisfying. Your vegetarian guests will be thrilled. Just halve the recipe for a smaller crowd.

Yield: 24 servings

Vinaigrette:
1 cup olive oil
1 cup white balsamic vinegar
4 teaspoons granulated garlic
Sea salt and ground black pepper to taste
2 teaspoons Dijon mustard

Salad:
6 (15.5-oz.) cans cannellini beans, drained and rinsed

4 red bell peppers, chopped
1 red onion, chopped
4 tablespoons basil leaves, cut into thin strips
2 tablespoons chopped fresh oregano leaves
2 tablespoons fresh thyme leaves
2 tablespoons capers

Vinaigrette: Combine ingredients for vinaigrette in a bowl; whisk well. Set aside to allow flavors to meld.

Salad: In a large bowl, combine beans, red bell peppers, red onion, herbs and capers. Toss to mix well. About 1 hour before serving, pour dressing over beans and mix well.

SWEET-AND-SOUR ITALIAN SLAW

The combination of crunch from cabbage, carrots and apple make this salad irresistible. Add to that the play of sour against sweet from two vinegars, piqued by just a hint of hot pepper, and you've got a slaw like no other. Personally, I like this on top of the grilled spiedie meat, with or without the Italian bread.

Yield: 24 servings

Dressing:
1 cup extra-virgin olive oil
1/2 cup white-wine vinegar
1/2 cup rice-wine vinegar
4 teaspoons granulated garlic
2 teaspoons dried oregano
2 teaspoons dried thyme

1 teaspoon red-pepper flakes
Salt and pepper to taste
Salad:
1 head green cabbage, thinly sliced
1 head purple cabbage, thinly sliced
8 medium carrots, peeled and grated
2 Granny Smith apples, peeled, cored and grated
6 green onions, white and green parts, thinly sliced
1 cup packed Italian parsley leaves, chopped

Dressing: Combine dressing ingredients in a bowl, whisking well. Set aside.

Salad: In a large bowl, combine cabbages, carrots, apple, green onion and parsley. Toss to mix. An hour before serving, whisk dressing again and pour over slaw mixture, tossing to mix well.

LAVENDER LEMON BARS

A great lemon bar is a joy to behold and to eat. Adding just a touch of lavender to the crust takes the taste experience to a new level. If you find lavender too assertive, cut back on the amount just a smidge.

Yield: 24 servings

Crust:
4 cups sifted flour
1 cup cold butter, grated
1 cup powdered sugar
4 teaspoons crushed lavender flowers, dried or fresh

Filling:
8 eggs
2 cups sugar
1 cup flour
2 teaspoons baking powder
1 cup freshly squeezed lemon juice (from 5 to 6 lemons)
2 tablespoons grated lemon zest (see note)
Powdered sugar for dusting

Crust: Preheat oven to 350°. Trace the outlines of two 9-by-13-inch baking pans on parchment paper and cut out the rectangles to line the bottoms of the pans.

In a bowl, combine flour, grated butter and powdered sugar. Mix well with hands until the mixture is pliable. Divide dough between the two pans and pat out evenly with your fingers to cover the bottom of the pan. Sprinkle lavender flowers evenly over the pastry. Bake for 20 minutes; remove from oven and allow to cool completely.

Filling and assembly: Preheat oven to 350°. In a large mixing bowl, beat eggs, then whisk in sugar until well combined.

Measure flour into a separate bowl and stir in baking powder; then stir this mixture into the egg-sugar mixture. Add lemon juice and zest and mix well.

Pour filling over cooled crust in the pans. Return to 350° oven and bake for 20 to 25 minutes, or until set. Allow to cool before cutting into squares and dusting with powdered sugar. Pack bars in layers with wax paper between them in tightly sealed container.

NOTE: Zest the lemons while still whole, before you cut them to juice them. A Microplane file grater is the absolute best tool for the zesting job, and 2 or 3 lemons should provide enough zest for the 2 tablespoons required.

THE TIPSY GYPSY

While some people yearn to run away with the circus, Marshall has threatened to take his spiedies on the road, selling them at festivals from a cart he wants to call the Tipsy Gypsy. So when we needed to fashion a cocktail for our Italian-themed menu, the perfect name was already on the tips of our tongues. This is much like sangria but tweaked with the Italian liqueur called Tuaca, for a blend of brandy, citrus and vanilla that works perfectly in a wine cocktail. You'll find blood-orange juice — which gives the cocktail its striking color — in the grocery store alongside bottled orange and grapefruit juices.

Yield: 24 (6-oz.) cocktails

4 (750-ml) bottles dry rosé wine
3 cups blood-orange juice
1/2 cup Tuaca
1/4 cup fresh lime juice
1 pint fresh raspberries or sliced strawberries
Blood-orange-flavored sparkling water
Orange slices, cut into fourths, for garnish
Lime slices, cut into fourths, for garnish
Extra raspberries or strawberries, for garnish

Evenly divide the rosé, juices, Tuaca and raspberries or strawberries between 2 large pitchers or jars. Stir to combine. Cover and refrigerate overnight, stirring occasionally, allowing flavors to develop.

Before transferring to drink dispenser, strain out the fruit (it will have broken down in the alcohol overnight). You can add fresh strawberry and lime slices, if you like, at this point. At serving time, pour over ice in glasses, top with a splash of sparkling water and garnish with citrus and a raspberry or strawberry.

•••

Logistics: Get the spiedie meat into the marinade the day before and transport it to the tailgate in the sealed container you used to marinate it in; then skewer the meat on-site as you're waiting for the grill to heat up. You can make the bean salad and the dressing the night before and add the dressing to the salad in the morning before you pack it. Transfer the reserved dressing for the spiedies and the balsamic vinegar for the caprese skewers into squeeze bottles for ease of application at the site.

Don't forget: Fuel for the grill; small bowls for cocktail garnishes. If you have lavender blooms left after making the lemon bars, it would be lovely to cut some stems, wrap the ends in damp paper toweling for transport and then unwrap them on site and use them to garnish the lemon bars on the tailgate table.

CHILLY SATURDAY

Texas Chili for a Crowd
Yellow Cornbread, Sweet or Spicy
Sunny Seven-Layer Dip
Roasted-Tomato Salsa
Spicy Chocolate Brownies
Cocktail: Mango-Mint Margaritas

While much of the football season can be pretty warm in Texas, we can usually count on the last home game in November to be nice and cool. That's chili weather to us, and it's possibly my favorite time to tailgate. We make a giant batch of chili, usually the Texas variety — that's sans beans, of course. We serve cornbread with our chili, but you'll please the crowd if you set up your buffet with offerings of Fritos, grated cheddar cheese and chopped onion (or pico de gallo) so guests can create their own Frito chili pie, if they so please (see *Logistics* below). What could be more Texan than that?

TEXAS CHILI FOR A CROWD

When chili is on the menu, we know we'll have a big crowd, so we make plenty. You can stretch the servings by adding pinto beans, if you're not a Texas purist who is horrified by such heresy. If you opt for beans, 4 to 5 (15-oz.) cans should do it; just be sure to rinse the beans before adding them to the pots about 30 minutes before the chili will be removed from the heat. You can always prepare this chili in a large slow cooker, too: Brown onions, garlic and meat first in a separate skillet, skim off excess fat and transfer to slow cooker; set on LOW for 5 to 6 hours.

Yield: 25 to 30 servings

2 tablespoons olive oil
4 medium yellow onions, chopped
8 cloves garlic, minced
8 pounds ground beef
8 cups crushed tomatoes in tomato puree
1 to 1 1/2 cups Pendery's San Antonio Red Chile Blend (see note)
Sea salt to taste

Divide oil and onions between two large Dutch ovens over medium heat, sautéing until softened. Add garlic, sautéing until just softened.

Raise heat to medium-high and divide ground beef between the pans, stirring and browning for about 10 minutes. Stir in crushed tomatoes, dividing evenly, and reduce heat to medium-low. Simmer, uncovered, stirring occasionally, for 10 to 15 minutes; then divide chile powder between the pots and stir well. Cover and simmer, stirring occasionally, for 2 to 3 hours. Skim off excess fat before serving. Add salt to taste.

NOTE: Pendery's, whose founder began marketing the first commercially sold chili seasoning in the late 1800s, still sells that original blend, Chiltomaline – along with hundreds of other spices and spice blends, many involving ground chiles. Pendery's San Antonio blend is our favorite for chili, mild enough for most palates and worth ordering at penderys.com. (If you're in the Fort Worth area, the store

— one of the region's most venerable and storied businesses — is worth a visit at 1407 Eighth Ave.) Acceptable alternatives includes the Whole Foods Market house brand and the Chili Mix seasoning from Bolner's Fiesta Brand, based in San Antonio and available at grocery stores across Texas and beyond.

YELLOW CORNBREAD, SWEET OR SPICY

Sweet or not? That's the discussion we have in our household. Marshall likes sweet cornbread; I'm the one who wants my cornbread sans sugar. Some folks don't want their cornbread spicy, either, so we make a double batch — one sweet, one spicy — to suit everyone. Splitting the batter in half, we add sugar to one bowl and minced jalapeños to the other bowl, and everyone's happy. Of course, if you like sweet and spicy cornbread, you can just throw it all together. We like to cook our cornbread in cast iron, using two large (at least 15-inch) skillets, but you can also make it in two 9-by-13-inch baking pans.

Yield: 24 servings

1 stick (1/2 cup) unsalted butter
4 cups all-purpose flour
4 cups yellow cornmeal
2 tablespoons baking powder
2 teaspoons sea salt
8 large eggs
2 cups buttermilk
2 cups half-and-half
1/4 cup sugar

1 large jalapeño, seeded, minced

Heat oven to 400°. Divide the butter evenly between two large cast-iron skillets or two 9-by-13-inch pans and place pans in the oven. When butter is melted, remove pans (keep oven on) and brush the melted butter up the sides of the pans.

Meanwhile, in a large bowl, whisk together flour, cornmeal, baking powder and sea salt. In another bowl, lightly whisk eggs and add buttermilk and half-and half, whisking well to combine.

Make a well in the center of the dry mixture and stir in the wet ingredients. Gently stir to combine all ingredients without overmixing.

Pour half the batter back into the other bowl and add minced jalapeño to that bowl. Add sugar to the first bowl, stirring both well to combine. Pour each batter into a prepared pan and bake for 20 to 25 minutes, or until top is a deep golden-brown and a toothpick inserted in center comes away clean. Cool and cut into serving pieces.

SUNNY SEVEN-LAYER DIP

This variation on a classic is customized to our tastes. Black beans take the place of refrieds on the bottom layer to provide texture (and they're healthier, for those keeping score at home). Guacamole tops the beans, followed by roasted corn cut from the cob (or thawed frozen corn, if fresh isn't available). Next, sour cream is topped by salsa verde, which provides a tart flavor pop from tomatillos (find the Herdez brand if you can). Grated cheeses cover the salsa, and pico de gallo, in the colors of the Mexican flag, is the crowning touch. We deleted the customary slices of black olives because we just don't find them that interesting. This striking layered dip looks best in a clear serving bowl to show off its colorful strata. You'll need either a very large bowl or two medium-large ones. Be sure you have plenty of sturdy tortilla chips on hand for dipping. There's no meat here, so those who prefer not to enjoy the chili can turn to this as their main dish — even though it's technically a dip, it's quite substantial.

Yield: 28 to 32 servings

6 ears corn, kernels cut from the cob
4 to 6 teaspoons olive oil
Sea salt to taste
4 medium or 3 large tomatoes, diced
2 medium yellow onions, diced
2 jalapeños, seeded, diced
1 cup cilantro leaves, chopped
Juice of 2 limes
8 large, ripe avocados
Juice of 2 lemons
2 teaspoons granulated garlic
Several dashes Valentina or Cholula hot sauce, to taste
4 (15-oz.) cans black beans, rinsed and drained
3 cups tomatillo-based salsa verde
16 oz. sour cream
2 cups grated sharp cheddar cheese
2 cups grated monterey jack cheese
Tortilla chips for dipping

Preheat oven to 350°. Toss corn kernels with just enough olive oil to lightly coat them and with sea salt to taste in a long baking dish or pan. Roast uncovered, stirring once, for 10 minutes or until just starting to brown. Remove from oven and allow to cool completely.

Meanwhile, in a bowl, make pico de gallo by combining diced tomatoes and onion, jalapeños and chopped cilantro with lime juice. Set aside.

In another bowl, make guacamole by mashing avocadoes together with lemon juice and granulated garlic; add sea salt and hot sauce to taste.

In a very large clear serving bowl (or two bowls), spread black beans on bottom of dish for the first layer of dip. Spread guacamole gently over the black beans. Scatter roasted corn over the guacamole layer and top with sour cream. Next, layer the salsa verde over the sour cream and follow with mixed grated cheeses. Finish with pico de gallo.

ROASTED-TOMATO SALSA

Yes, there are dozens of fine ready-made salsas on the market. Right here in Fort Worth, Mrs. Renfro's and Joe T. Garcia's bottle excellent salsas for commercial sale all over the country. There's also a little cottage business here called Happy Tomato, where an enterprising young woman makes superb salsa that's now sold at Central Market and other Texas retailers. But I'm a fool for the fresh salsa Marshall and I make with tomatoes from our garden. Marshall grows beautiful Romas in our backyard, harvesting bushels at a time in peak season. We roast them in the oven, then puree these and freeze them by the gallon. That way we have roasted tomatoes for salsa and pasta sauce all year long. It's an easy process. Here's our salsa recipe; omit cilantro or substitute Italian parsley for it if you're a cilantro-frowner.

Yield: 1 gallon

36 to 40 Roma tomatoes, cut in half
2 to 3 fresh New Mexico green chiles
3 tablespoons olive oil, divided
2 medium yellow onions, roughly chopped
1 bunch cilantro leaves, roughly chopped, optional
Juice of 1 lemon
2 tablespoons ground cumin
2 tablespoons garlic granules
Sea salt to taste
Tortilla chips for dipping

Preheat oven to 375°. Line three large raised-rim baking sheets with parchment paper. Arrange tomato halves, cut side down, on two of the sheets and brush with 2 tablespoons of the olive oil. Place green chiles on the third baking sheet and brush with remaining 1 tablespoon olive oil.

Place sheets with tomatoes in oven and roast for 45 minutes to an hour, until peels are split and pulling away from the flesh. Remove from oven and set aside to cool. Raise temperature to 400° and roast chiles for 35 to 40 minutes, or until charred on all sides.

Transfer roasted tomatoes to food processor and puree until smooth. Transfer to a large bowl. Peel charred skins from green chiles and discard skins, along with stems and seeds. Finely chop green chiles and add to pureed tomatoes.

Combine onions and cilantro (if using) in processor and pulse until finely chopped; transfer to bowl with tomatoes and chiles. Stir in lemon juice, cumin, garlic granules and sea salt to taste, mixing well.

Taste and adjust seasonings. Serve with tortilla chips for dipping.

SPICY CHOCOLATE BROWNIES

This is a variation on a recipe from Ghirardelli, the company making the chocolate I prefer to use in baking, and it's perfect for the true chocoholic who likes a kick. In addition to two kinds of chocolate, there's cinnamon and cayenne in the mix. Modify the cayenne to suit your taste (or that of your guests). If you like a less-sweet brownie, use a bittersweet chocolate bar instead of semi-sweet. These make a delightful snack to be enjoyed with coffee, too.

Yield: 32 2-inch brownies

8 oz. semi-sweet chocolate baking bar, chopped
1 cup cold unsalted butter, cut into 1/2-inch cubes, plus 2 table-
    spoons butter at room temperature for pans
Flour for coating pans
2 cups firmly packed dark-brown sugar
2 teaspoons pure vanilla extract
4 large eggs, beaten lightly
1 1/2 cups plus 4 tablespoons all-purpose flour
1/2 teaspoon baking powder
1 teaspoon ground cinnamon
1/2 to 3/4 teaspoon ground cayenne pepper
1 teaspoon sea salt
1 cup semi-sweet chocolate baking chips

Using a large double boiler or a large heatproof mixing bowl set over
a pan of water, melt the chopped chocolate bar with the 1 cup cold

cubes of butter over gently simmering water, stirring occasionally, until melted and smooth. Remove from heat and allow to cool.

Meanwhile, preheat oven to 350°. Thoroughly grease two 8-inch square baking pans with 1 tablespoon each of room-temperature butter and dust lightly but thoroughly with flour, tapping pans to distribute evenly and to remove excess flour.

In a medium mixing bowl, thoroughly stir together brown sugar and vanilla. Add beaten eggs and stir until incorporated. Scrape this mixture into the cooled chocolate mixture and blend well.

Separately sift together flour, baking powder, cinnamon, cayenne and salt; add dry ingredients to the chocolate mixture and stir until blended. Stir in chocolate chips. Divide batter between the prepared pans.

Bake for 25 to 30 minutes or until a toothpick inserted at center comes away clean. Cool for 15 minutes before cutting into squares.

MANGO-MINT MARGARITAS

We serve margaritas at least once each season; we're in Texas, after all, and many of us will tell you the marg is one of Texas' gifts to the world. Margarita varieties are as plentiful as the fruits you can name. Thanks to the advent of frozen mango chunks in your grocery store's freezer section, this particular version is a whole lot easier to make than back when we had to peel fresh mangoes — a messy endeavor if there ever were one. Squeezing the limes takes some time but is well worth it; be sure to roll the limes with your palm on a cutting board, pushing down to loosen the juice inside, before cutting them in half. The best tool for juicing is that inexpensive handheld lime squeezer with the two lever handles and the cup that keeps any seeds inside it. We like to buy extra mango chunks and keep them frozen until the last minute, to float in our drink dispenser to keep the large batch cold.

Yield: About 25 (6-oz.) cocktails

12 cups frozen mango chunks, divided
3 cups fresh lime juice (from about 24 limes)
1 1/2 cups packed fresh mint leaves
1 liter silver tequila
Ice
Mint sprigs, for garnish
Lime wedges, for garnish

Hold back 4 cups of the frozen mango chunks in a zip-seal bag in the freezer to use in the drinks dispenser.

In a blender, puree remaining 8 cups of the frozen mango with the lime juice and the mint; you'll probably need to do this in batches. Keep mixture cold until time to add tequila in the drinks dispenser. At serving time, stir in tequila and add reserved frozen mango chunks. Serve cocktails over ice with mint and lime garnishes.

●●●

Logistics: We make most of this menu the day before, though the layered dip is best made the morning of the tailgate. Reheat chili at home before the tailgate; transfer to large foil pans, wrapping well with heavy foil, and transport in Cambro; keep warm at the tailgate in pans over Sterno. For the Frito pie contingent, arrange a self-serve assembly line near the chili with a big bowl of Fritos, a bowl of chopped onion and a bowl of grated cheddar. The cornbread is easiest to manage if you cut it into squares in advance and transport them in heavy-duty plastic ware; ditto for the brownies.

Don't forget: Labels for the sweet and spicy cornbread so your guests will know which is which. You'll need two or three large bags of tortilla chips for the two dips; we like the Juanita's, Santitas, Julio's, Mission, Xochitl and El Milagro brands (as we mentioned earlier, don't open them all at once; unseal the bags as needed to maintain freshness). Be sure to retrieve the frozen mango chunks from the freezer to chill the margarita mixture, transporting them in plastic bags on ice in a cooler, and to pack the mint and lime garnishes. Pack bowls and spoons for chili, as well as ingredients and bowls for Frito pie: a large bag of the original smaller Fritos (not the larger dipping ones), a cup or two of chopped yellow onion and about 2 cups of shredded sharp cheddar.

ABOUT THE AUTHORS

June Naylor Harris and Marshall K. Harris both graduated from Fort Worth's Texas Christian University in 1979, and their loyalty to the Horned Frogs is exceeded only by their passion for cooking.

June's career spans that of dining critic, food writer and recipe developer, working for such publications as the *Fort Worth Star-Telegram, Dallas Morning News, 360 West* and *Texas Monthly*. She is also a travel writer and *Texas Highways* contributing editor. Her cookbooks include *Big Ranch, Big City* (Ten Speed Press, $40), co-authored with fellow TCU alum Louis Lambert, and the popular *Texas Landmark Cafes* for Great Texas Line Press ($5.95, greattexasline.com).

Early in her career, she wrote about sports, landing her first *Star-Telegram* byline in 1984 with a story about fellow Horned Frog Marshall Harris, former TCU football star who was leaving the NFL to play for the fledgling USFL.

Three decades later, Marshall and June became husband and wife. They live in Fort Worth, where Marshall enjoys a successful studio art practice (marshallkharris.com) and presides over a bountiful garden. They are honored to have taken the reins of Marshall's parents' longtime tailgate tradition at TCU, where Marshall and his father are the only father-son inductees in the TCU Lettermen's Hall of Fame.

Texas White Trash Cookbook

"Everything your Memaw should have taught y'all" – Lou Hudson, author of *Speak Texan in 30 Minutes or Less*
Betty Ann Stout is back, sharing cooking secrets of her Mamma and her great aunts and regular aunts and her Memaw and other people's aunts and memaws and mammas and a daddy or uncle or three.
96 pages. Paperback. ISBN 9781-1-892588-647. List $5.95

Celebrations from a Cowgirl's Kitchen:
Texas Fiestas, Fandangos & Feasts

"Entertaining and enticing" – *San Angelo Standard-Times*
"Awesome! Garner's recipes reflect eclectic sensibility." – *AAA Texas Journey Magazine*
Texas native Christine Gardner rounds up 11 menus for festive Texas-style occasions from casual to luxe, offering cowgirl entertaining with ease and style.
144 pages. Paperback, ISBN 978-1892588-371. List $7.50

Cordon Bubba: Texas Downhome Cooking

"Just perfect" – *Wichita Falls Times Record News*
"A tiny treasure" – *Sherman Herald-Democrat*
Easy-to-follow, genuine Lone Star recipes, from calf fries and real Texas barbecue sauce to chicken-fried steak to award-winning chili con carne, King Ranch chicken, fajitas, cheese grits and sweet potato pie.
80 pages. Paperback. ISBN 978-1-892588-005. List $5.95

Texas Landmark Cafes

Also by June Naylor Harris, a perfect guide for people hoping to avoid homogenized chain food and discover some great eats wherever they travel in Texas. '"This pocket-size gem focuses on Naylor's favorite dining spots in small towns and big cities," raves the *Houston Chronicle*.
88 Pages. Paperback. ISBN 9781-1892588-17-X. List $5.95